Garden of Earthly Delights

– LESLEY GOULD –

lesley Gould.

Printed and bound in England by www.printondemand-worldwide.com

http://www.fast-print.net/bookshop

GARDEN OF EARTHLY DELIGHTS
Copyright © Lesley Gould 2016

A catalogue record for this book is available from the British Library

ISBN 978-178456-407-0

First published 2016 by
FASTPRINT PUBLISHING
Peterborough, England

Garden of Earthly Delights – a short tour of China

Introduction

From school all I remember about China was that the people grow and eat a lot of rice and I imagine pictures of people working in rice terraces and fields, wearing Coolie hats. It wasn't that my education was poor but rather that at the time China was a closed country and not one that was on the exam syllabus so you didn't learn about it. I also knew a little about blue and white pottery and that some of this came from China and I knew The Willow Pattern Story because I owned a book with the story in it. I also remember pictures of blossom trees and people in traditional Chinese clothes. Today we all know a lot more about the country, it is often in the news and with instant access to information we can immediately research facts. It seems though that however much you learn about China it only increases the amount of information you don't know. Having read many authors accounts of people growing up in China both before and during the cultural revolution it has created a real thirst to see China first hand. I have included a glossary at the back with details of books that I found interesting. Some are actual accounts and others are fiction set in times and places that give a lot of background information about China and the countries surrounding it, and as such are

3

interesting social histories. All are very readable. It was only recently that I was reading a wonderful book by Tan Twan Eng, where I discovered how badly the Chinese were treated by the Japanese when they invaded China during WW2. We hear a lot about the occupation of Singapore but I had never really considered how the war affected the Chinese population. It was a real eye opener.

It has always been rather a secretive country and it is only relatively recently that the western world has been

able to gain more of an insight into its everyday life. A short tour of China was only going to give a snapshot but it gave a feel for the place and a chance to delve beneath the surface of what I knew or expected. It was a chance to form my own opinions and thoughts even if restricted in what I saw. I had advice from friends and acquaintances who had been before me but I was really looking forward to forming my own opinions and experiencing it firsthand.

China is reputed to be one of the oldest continuous civilisations in the world. Its unique culture and customs make it appear an amazingly interesting place to visit. Before arriving I wanted to find out some facts about the country.

Its full name is The People's Republic of China and it covers 3,706,580 square miles. Its capital is Beijing and the current population (2016) is over 1.38 billion. This compares with the population of the UK being 65 million. The Chinese People are the largest nationality in the world. There are over 160 cities in China with a population of over 1 million people. It is the fourth largest country in the world by area. It is made up of 23 provinces, 5 autonomous regions, 4 municipalities, and two Special Administrative Regions.

The Chinese refer to their country as the Middle Kingdom, an indication of how central they have felt themselves to be throughout history. There are cultural and linguistic variations in different regions, but for such a large country the culture is relatively uniform. However, fifty-five minority groups inhabit the more remote regions of the country and have their own unique cultures, languages, and customs.

The Yangtze is the longest river in the country and forms the official dividing line between north and south China. The Yangtze sometimes floods badly, as does the Yellow River to the north, which, because of the damage it has caused, is called "China's sorrow."

The country is divided into two regions: Inner China and Outer China. Historically, the two have been very separate. The Great Wall, which was built in the fifteenth century to protect the country against military invasions, marks the division. While the areas of the two regions are roughly equal, 95 percent of the population lives in Inner China. The land has higher plateaus and mountainous areas in the west, moving to the lower plains and then the flat coastal areas in the east.

Chinese people speak mandarin which is based on Beijing Dialect. Their written language is obviously very different to ours. The formation of Chinese characters has a history of more than 3,000 years. The writing system is the same for all the dialects. It is complex and difficult to learn and consists of almost sixty thousand characters, although only about five thousand are used in everyday life. This makes Chinese particularly difficult to learn. Unlike other modern languages, which use phonetic alphabets, Chinese is written in pictographs and ideographs, symbols that represent concepts rather than sounds. Chinese is also a tonal language meaning that words are differentiated not just by sounds but by whether the intonation is rising or falling. How a character is written can also give it a different meaning making it doubly difficult.

The flag has a red background with a yellow star in the upper left-hand corner and four smaller yellow stars in a crescent formation to its right.  The colour red symbolizes the revolution. The large star stands for the Communist Party, and the four small stars symbolize the Chinese people. The position of the stars stands for a populace united in support of the state.

The standard time is used throughout the country and is eight hours ahead of us in Britain. It is called Beijing Time but does not refer to Beijing, instead it is the time taken in Lintong District, Shaanxi Province whose longitude is 116 degrees east, the geometric centre of the country. It is handy though not having to change time zones in the country. I remember crossing several time zones when visiting Canada.

The country is home to several endangered species, including the giant panda, the golden monkey, several species of tiger, the Yangtze alligator, and the red-crowned crane. While outside organizations such as the World Wildlife Fund have made efforts to save these animals, their preservation is not a top priority for the government.

There are several panda breeding programmes though including one in Chengdu near to Xian which was set up in 1987 dedicated to the conservation of the giant panda.

The main symbol of the nation is the dragon, a fantastical creature made up of seven animals. It is accorded the power to change its size at will and to bring the rain that farmers need. New Year's festivities often include a line of people in a dragon costume.

It is one of the earliest places where society originated entering its Imperial stage in the 21st century BC. There were many Dynasties and wars until The People's Republic of China was set up in 1949.

According to the Law on Nationality, China does not recognise dual nationality for any of its citizens. If a Chinese citizen has another citizenship of a foreign country, the Chinese citizenship he possesses will be automatically invalid.

Nowadays though, Chinese people enjoy a higher standard of living, with greatly improved facilities for education which contributes much to the overall quality of life for the entire nation. Economic growth means that in time even the poorer regions will enjoy a higher standard of living but with such a large population these improvements take time. There has been a distinct improvement in the status of women and rights of senior citizens and children enjoy more protection and care. Chinese society has become more open, accommodating and self-sustaining in these new times. However, the people never forget to carry forward and develop the traditional Chinese virtues. I found this time after time.

To me China seemed to be an ancient, mysterious and beautiful land that appealed to my sense of adventure and I couldn't wait to visit it. I had done as much research as possible about the places I was visiting all I had to do now was travel there. A full itinerary is given in the pages at the back of the book.

So there I was, on a sunny spring afternoon, travelling

alone on a train to St Pancras, London, on the first leg of my journey to China. Off to start a tour that began in Shanghai.

I was travelling with China Eastern for both the international flights and the three internal flights. I wasn't apprehensive as they have a very good safety record but they have had a lot of negative reviews from foreign travellers.

The logo on the plane depicts a phoenix, a legendary bird worshipped by the nation since ancient times and a symbol of luck and happiness.

All I can say is that my experience was great. The staff were all friendly and helpful, food was as good as any airline food is in economy. The only down side for me was that in the morning I didn't fancy Chinese food for breakfast, but that was me, not the fault of the airline. They did have hot rolls and coffee so all was well. You can't complain when a national airline serves its own food and the majority of the travellers were Asian. It was a long flight being eleven hours going out and over thirteen hours on the return. The flight home seemed particularly long as I had to fly from Beijing to Shanghai first.

However I arrived in Shanghai about 5pm in the evening and was met by my Chinese guides Dave and Lim, and then transferred to the Ocean Hotel. I didn't have long to unpack as I was due out for dinner at 7pm. I had a lovely large double room, with a walk in wet room and a bath. It was on the 13th floor so also had good views across the city and you could see some of the huge buildings in the Pudong area. One evening I went up to the 27th floor where they had a revolving restaurant with great views over the city.

It was a modern hotel and very comfortable. I found that it was very central too making travel times shorter when visiting sites.

The Bund

Shanghai sits at the mouth of the Yangtze River, the longest river in China. It is the largest Chinese city and "a city of skyscrapers". With a history of more than 700 years, Shanghai was once the financial centre of the Far East. Today, Shanghai is the largest economic and transportation centre in China. The municipal government is working towards building Shanghai into a modern metropolis and into a world economic, financial, trading and shipping centre.

Shanghai has become a first stop for many overseas visitors. The architecture here is another landscape totally. The Bund with the old Shanghai-style buildings has a huge variety of architectural styles derived from combinations of local and origin culture. There are modern shopping malls and back street lanes, dazzling antiques and Chinese folk art. So I was there at last.

My first outing in Shanghai was at dusk to The Bund. I left the hotel and dinner was booked at a small restaurant by the river in this well known famous area.

The buildings were just beginning to light up and it was looking quite impressive then, but nothing like its neon glory that hit me as I came out of the restaurant later. Across the river in Pudong Park, the skyline area was totally lit up. On the buildings the colours and shapes were changing all the time. Cruise boats were lit up and moving up and down the river so visitors could look at the buildings and the sights and in doing so became part of the scene. It was very impressive.

One of the most outstanding buildings because of its incredible shape is the Oriental TV Tower. The Tower, in Pudong Park, is surrounded by the Yangpu Bridge and the Nanpu Bridge. In the daytime this creates a picture of two dragons playing with pearls. The entire area is a photographic jem that attracts thousands of visitors all year.

The tower is 1,536 feet high and is the world's sixth and China's second tallest TV and radio tower. However, it is not its height but the unique architectural design that makes the Oriental Pearl TV Tower one of the most attractive and interesting places. Its base is supported by three seven-metre wide slanting stanchions. Then eleven steel spheres are 'strung' vertically through the centre of the tower surrounded by three columns. The large sphere at the top is known as the space module. Then there are five smaller spheres and three decorative spheres on the tower base.

When you visit you travel up and down the tower in double-decker elevators that can hold up to fifty people at a time and travels at seven meters per second. The elevator attendants give you an introduction to the TV Tower in English and Chinese during the rapid 1/4-mile ascent. Once you reach your stop there are a variety of different facilities.

The Shanghai Municipal History Museum is located within it. The large lower sphere has a futuristic space city and a fabulous sightseeing hall. From here, on a clear day you can see all the way to the Yangtze River. The base of the tower is like a science fantasy city. The five smaller spheres are actually a hotel that contains twenty-five rooms. The pearl at the very top contains shops, restaurants, (including a rotating restaurant) and a sightseeing floor. The view of Shanghai from this height is amazing when the weather is clear. When viewed from the Bund at night, the tower's three-dimensional lighting makes it stand out in brilliant colour.

It's hard to remember it really is a TV and radio tower that services the Shanghai area with more than nine television channels and upwards of ten FM radio channels.

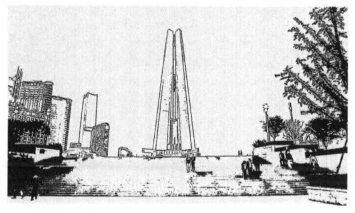

The Bund which actually means the embankment, refers to Shanghai's famous waterfront running along the shore of the Huangpu River. It forms the boundary of old downtown Shanghai. Once it was just a muddy towpath for boats along the river and was where the foreign powers that came to Shanghai with the International Settlement, built their distinct Western-style banks and trading houses. It was because of this that Shanghai grew into Asia's leading city in the 1920s and 1930s, becoming a thriving commercial and financial centre.

Many of the wonderful old and ostentatious colonial structures that today are still there date from that prosperous time. They are now a well known part of Shanghai's cityscape.

Some of the buildings which stand out include the former British Consulate, the Customs House, the former Hong Kong and Shanghai Bank, the old Shanghai Club which is now the Waldorf Astoria Hotel, and the Peace Hotel. Most of these buildings have now been skillfully restored as the Chinese government, when preparing for the 2010 World Expo, spent a lot of money renovating the Bund. So today it has regained much of its previous glory. A four-lane road now runs in front of these old buildings. On the river side of the road there is a 2.6km-long (1.6-mile) raised promenade, with new trees and benches allowing visitors pleasant strolls along the river and marvellous views of both the Bund and Pudong Park across the river.

After dinner I strolled along this river walkway. There were lots of photographers taking photographs. Many of these were of couples having their wedding photographs taken with The Pudong skyline as the backdrop. It is common to do this in China so that many of these formalities are out if the way before the big day. Also most of the brides wore red as this is a lucky and auspicious colour for the Chinese. It felt a bit like walking through a film set. There weren't just a few but lots of them.

It was only a generation ago that most marriages were arranged by parents or by a professional matchmaker. Weddings are big affairs and huge amounts of money out of all proportion to salaries are spent on this. I happened one day to be dining in a restaurant where a wedding meal was taking place and was given flowers and had my photograph taken with the bride. They were very welcoming to the fact that I was European and therefore a novelty!

The Pudong across the river is the modern face of Shanghai. The Shanghai Stock Exchange and many of Shanghai's best-known buildings, such as the Oriental Pearl Tower, the Jin Mao Tower, the Shanghai World Financial Centre, and the Shanghai Tower are all found here. These modern skyscrapers directly face the historic Bund. It is all very H-i tech and Sci- Fi looking. These are the buildings and the skyline that most people recognise as Shanghai and it is this that dominates the area after dark. Along the walkway as well there is a statue of a bull which is lit up and is the symbol of the Shanghai Stock Exchange.

For years though it was the Bund that was the first sight of Shanghai for those arriving by boat and it was my first stop as well. So my first day ended in ultra modern style, dining and meandering in modern Shanghai but with a strong link to the past. I retired to a very comfortable bed ready for an early start in the morning. Tomorrow was going to be a great contrast to this evening.

The Yu Gardens

After an early wake- up call and breakfast it was off to visit an older part of Shanghai City.

It was a gorgeous hot day in Shanghai, one of the clearest they get when I visited the Yu Gardens, which was the private garden of the Pan family. It is found in the centre of Shanghai's Old City, only a few blocks away from the Bund and it covers an area of about five acres.

The Yuyuan Garden is believed to have been built more than 400 years ago in the Ming Dynasty. The layout, the beautiful plants and flowers and the artistic style of the garden have made it a brilliant place to visit while in Shanghai.

It is important and revered as it is the only surviving Ming Dynasty garden in Shanghai. It is a stunning example of what a traditional Chinese Garden

is, including all the four elements, which are plants, water, stone and buildings. They are intended to portray serenity and beauty and they were certainly that.

Upon entering the garden, you come across a rockery, which is called the Great Rockery. It is about fifty feet high and is the largest as well as the oldest rockery in the southern region of the Yangtze River. It is a quiet and elegant place surrounded by old trees and beautiful flowers.

It was built by Pan Yunduan for his parents as they got old, as in the traditional Chinese way the children always look after and respect the elder members of their family. Yu in Chinese means pleasing and satisfying. He wanted his parents to spend a quiet and happy life in their old age. He first thought of making it in 1559, but the building of it was delayed as he was transferred to Sichuan for almost twenty years. He returned to Shanghai in 1577 to start the project.

The story ends quite sadly as only a few years after the garden was completed, his parents passed away. Also as he had spent a great amount of money on the construction of the garden, in his later life he had to sell some of his lands and antiques due to his circumstances.

It was a lovely hot, sunny morning when I visited and being spring there was lots of colour and blossom. As well as the garden itself there are buildings and halls and some original furniture, art work, decorative bridges, pagodas and inscriptions. It is such an atmospheric place to visit as everywhere you look there is something else to catch the eye and the attention to detail is mesmerising. There are many intimate areas separated by dragon walls and many sculptures arches and moon gates. Everything here has a reason or meaning, for example a square room represents earth and a round room would represent heaven.

One of the highlights of the garden is the Exquisite Jade Rock. The rock is characterized by its wrinkled appearance, and numerous holes eroded by water. It appears almost translucent in some light. An interesting legend goes that the rock was actually found 1000 years ago, and it originally belonged to Emperor Huizong.

However it now resides in the Yu Garden.

The garden was later inherited by Zhang Zhaolin - Pan Yunduan's granddaughter's husband. Then later still it was split up by other people not relevant to his family.

The buildings are designed as those of a typical Chinese house. The pavilions were as important as the garden. Originally the windows would not have had glass in them but rice paper or silk which was intricately decorated by the women in the house. The women rarely ventured outside the house area and had lots of time to work on these. It was also a way of showing their love for the family as love was something that the Chinese never spoke out loud. Instead it was shown in actions. It had a reception room where guests were greeted, living and sleeping quarters, an area for the daughter of the family and areas where plays or operas were held.

 Wandering around the garden is like entering small scenes in a play. At each turn you find something new and

interesting to look at and photograph. You cannot help but be awed by the attention to detail.

There are many old trees in the garden and one newer one. This was where the Camphor tree had been planted when Yunduans daughter was born but which would have been chopped down according to Chinese custom when she married to make a wooden box for her wedding dowry. It was then replaced by a new tree.

Leaving the garden you pass through a bazaar with lots of shops and stall where you can buy or haggle for almost anything. At the end of this you enter Old

Shanghai City. Although not all old themselves the buildings are all in the old style and very attractive. As well as being able to buy anything there are lots of food

outlets, dumpling houses and fast food. Also here is the famous Huxinting teahouse built in 1784. The zig-zag bridge is supposed to protect the structure because it was believed that evil spirits can only go in straight lines and not turn corners.

There is a lovely feel about this place. It blends old and new very easily. Traditional buildings house modern shops including Starbucks coffee. Alongside this there was a lot of street food being prepared and several arts and craft stalls with the artists working as well as selling. I bought a lovely ink painting from one of the artists here. It was a picture of a hillside and  waterfalls done only with his nails, which he used as brushes with the black ink. In retrospect I should have bargained on the price but I was new to it then! There is a real mix of people here, old and young but mainly Chinese. During the whole tour I saw very few foreign groups.

Tea

The next thing I did in Shanghai after visiting the Yuyuan Garden and shopping was to go to a tea tasting. I had been up early and was ready for a cup of tea, or two!

Tea is an indispensable part of people's daily life in China. Although coffee shops have mushroomed in recent years many Chinese people still prefer to relax at

a teahouse. In Shanghai there are over 3,000 teahouses providing a wide range of choices to appreciate the charm of the varied Chinese tea culture. I suppose it's like our current cafe culture except theirs goes back many years.

There are many old and famous teahouses gathered around Shanghai Old Street. Most of them are decorated in an ancient Chinese style. They serve excellent Chinese tea as well as simple local food and snacks. My experience was that they were also doing a roaring trade.

On entering there were lots of different teas available to try and a great list of their medicinal properties. These claims were many and varied. I was amazed at the visual effects of some of the teas. We tried a beautiful Jasmine tea that looked just like a type of seed or bulb, but when the water was added the flower grew from this and looked beautiful in the pot. You definitely need a clear teapot to view this. I actually bought some of these not from the tea tasting shop but found them in a tea shop in Wuzhen. I have been using them in a cafetière after meals to impress guests. The tea is also very pleasant, not too floral or vegetal.

The health benefits of jasmine tea are said to reduce the risk of heart attacks, to strengthen the immune system, and help prevent of diabetes. Some also claim that Jasmine tea helps prevent cancer, reduces stress, improves digestive processes, and lowers cholesterol. It has been found to eliminate harmful bacteria and ease chronic inflammation like muscle aches and pains. Worth a try definitely!

Jasmine tea is not considered a "herbal tea", because it is actually normal tea that is flavoured with jasmine flowers to create the unique scent and taste. I am quite a convert to it.

China is one of the most important tea-producing countries. The written history of tea consumption in China goes back longer than in any other country. In ancient China, tea was originally used as a medicine and over hundreds of years it slowly shifted towards being viewed first as a tonic, and then as the beverage that it is today. Most of the tea produced in China is consumed in China, although tea is also an important export.

The importance and fascination with tea led me to wonder how tea actually originated. According to legend, tea was first discovered by a Chinese Emperor and herbalist, Shennong. It is said that the emperor liked his drinking water boiled before he drank it so it would be clean. One day, on a trip to a distant region, he and his army stopped to rest. A servant began boiling water for him to drink and a dead leaf from the wild tea bush fell into the water. It turned a brownish colour, but no one had noticed this and the drink was presented to the emperor. The emperor drank it and found it very refreshing, and tea came into being.

The French Concession Area

Following this I was taken to the area known as The French Concession. This is the area of Shanghai once designated for the French, and is today an extremely popular shopping and dining spot for tourists. It is also very close to the Shanghai Stadium.

 The tree-lined avenues and the large mansions in the area give it a very Parisienne feel and it certainly has its own distinct character. There are many trendy cafes here and lots of interesting, though quite expensive shops. It feels wrong to haggle here though I am told it is perfectly acceptable.

The Shanghai   French   Concession was   a   foreign concession in Shanghai from 1849 until 1943. The concession came to an end in 1943 when the French government signed   it   over   to   the   pro-Japanese government   in Nanjing. For   much of the 20th century, the area covered by the former French Concession

remained the premier residential and retail district of Shanghai.

It wasn't just the French but the USA, UK, Russia, Italy, Austria-Hungary, Japan and Germany were all given territorial concessions across the city during the nineteenth century.

Walking around the area there are upmarket, pedestrian only shopping areas, eating venues and entertainment. There are many narrow alleys and stone paved courtyards. With its stone gate buildings, it is a beautiful area, and you could spend a whole morning here browsing through book shops, cafes and delis selling French cheese and wine. To the south of this area is the Site of the First National Congress of the Communist Party of China, which has now been preserved as a museum. Entry is free so if you have time, take a visit.

If you happen to arrive at Fuxing Park while wandering in this area make sure you go in. The gardens are wonderful, where mainly older people do tai chi around every corner. There are spontaneous ballroom dancers, mahjong and card enthusiasts, it's a real interesting mix.

Near the park is the Shanghai Sun Yat-Sen's Former Residence which is now a museum. Sun Yat-Sen was the forerunner of the Chinese democratic revolution and the founder of the Republic of China. The museum contains the original furnishings used by the family as well as displays of Mr. Sun Yat-Sen's activities from his stay in Shanghai.

Much of Shanghai's past beauty remains in this area, although many of the old buildings are in a desperate state of disrepair. It has a very safe feeling and appears quite European compared to most of Shanghai. There was some filming going on when I was there and it has been the backdrop to many films and TV programmes. There is certainly a very different feel to this area of Shanghai.

The Shanghai International Settlement originated following the defeat of the Qing dynasty of China by the British Empire in the First Opium War (1839–1842) and the signing of the Treaty of Nanking. Under the terms of the treaty, the Chinese city of Shanghai, along with four other treaty ports could now be open to foreign trade. The British, already active in Hong Kong, which had been ceded to them under the Treaty of Nanking, quickly established a settlement along the banks of the Whangpoo River to enable them to promote their commercial interests.

American and French involvement followed closely on the heels of the British, with distinct areas of settlement for the French in the south and the Americans to the north. In 1854, the three countries created the Shanghai Municipal Council to serve all their interests, but in 1862, the French concession dropped out of the arrangement. The following year the British and American settlements formally united to create the Shanghai International Settlement.

As more foreign powers entered into treaty relations with China, their nationals also became part of the administration of the settlement, but it always remained a predominantly British affair, at least until the late

1930s when Japan's involvement became of increasing importance.

The international settlement came to an abrupt end in December 1941 when Japanese troops stormed in immediately following the attack on Pearl Harbour. In early 1943, new treaties signed by Chiang Kai-shek's free Chinese government with Britain and the United States brought to an end the extraterritorial privileges which had been enjoyed by British subjects and American citizens for one hundred years.

In The French Concession area many of Shanghai's courtyard alleyways and lanes can be found. These are known as nongtangs, and are back passageways that combine traditional architectural design with modern Western architecture, giving an atmosphere that you will find in very few other places. These nongtangs have been around since the 1920s, and many of their original inhabitants still live there.

When you socialize with these local elderly residents they give accounts of the past and their stories of everyday life that show you the influence of Shanghai's development on their lifestyle. These local residents also often own small food markets located along these pathways. So you often find hidden stores.

As a visitor these older parts of cities hold far more interest than the newer ones. You can almost feel the atmosphere and the history.

The Nanjing Road

Again lunch was in a local restaurant. Although told what certain foods were these were often added to during the meal so I wasn't always sure what I was eating. It was mainly delicious, though there were a few odd flavours, just different to my palate I suppose.

Chicken feet are a part of the chicken that is cooked in China. It is a speciality here. Most of the edible tissue on the feet is the skin and tendons so there is no muscle and this gives the feet a distinct texture different from the rest of the chicken's meat. Their many small bones though do make them difficult to eat and these are often removed before serving. Being mostly skin, chicken feet are very gelatinous.

In China, and particularly in the south, there are snack bars specializing in marinated food such as duck's necks and chicken feet which are simmered with soy sauce, Sichuanese peppercorns, cloves and, garlic. Sometimes cinnamon and chili flakes are used. Today, packaged chicken feet are sold in most grocery stores and supermarkets in China as a snack, often seasoned with rice vinegar and chili. In southern China, they also cook chicken feet with raw peanuts to make a thin soup.

The huge demand in China has actually raised the price of chicken feet, which are often discarded in other countries. In June 2011, 1 kg of raw chicken feet cost around 12 to 16 yuan in China, compared to 11–12 yuan for 1 kg of frozen chicken breast. China is the major destination of chicken feet from around the globe.

After lunch I went exploring the Nanjing Road. Nanjing Road is the main shopping street of Shanghai and is one of the world's busiest shopping streets. The street is named after the city of Nanjing, capital of Jiangsu province which neighbours Shanghai. Today's Nanjing Road comprises two sections, Nanjing Road East and Nanjing Road West. Together these roads stretch close to ten kilometres.

The history of Nanjing Road can be traced back to the year 1845. At the beginning of the 20th century, eight big department stores became established along the street. A series of franchised stores were also set up at around that time.

However on 23 August 1937 a bomb was dropped on Nanjing Road by a Chinese plane in an attempt to lighten its load while being pursued by Japanese planes. The bomb hit two department stores, killing 612 people and injuring another 482.

In 2000, as a part of the development plan held by the local government, Nanjing Road was renovated and is now mainly a pedestrian street.

The Nanjing East Road is currently three kilometres of retail therapy with over 7,000 shops. Certainly walking along here it is all about the atmosphere. You could wander for hours admiring the buildings, the shop windows and just people watching. I spent a little while doing this but then decided to look down some of the side streets so wandered off down some of these. There were a lot of little alleyways off these side streets so it was easy to get lost. Again lots of shops but these were much smaller and in many ways more interesting.

As they were smaller the owners or salespeople were more available to chat and try to sell and bargain. It was beginning to come a little more naturally to me now, trying to get a bargain all the time! The side streets are perhaps more like how it would have been probably only forty or fifty years ago before big department stores took over.

Above the shops the washing was hanging out in the street and again there were lots of food outlets but also there were people approaching you to try and get you to go and visit their shops. Some were quite insistent but not to the point of worrying me, probably as there were plenty of other people around. I'm not so sure what it would feel like at night though.

I bought some children's chopsticks in a shop that sold

only chopsticks and elsewhere tried to bargain for a lovely leather wallet that was hand painted. I still regret not buying it as I never saw another. The most difficult part of shopping here was trying to cross a road and not get hit by a bike loaded with goods!

Jewish Links

From Nanjing Road I returned to the hotel and had some free time before going out for dinner and a river cruise. I decided to explore the area around the hotel as I hadn't yet had time to. I went down the side street rather than the busier Dondaming Road. There were lots of interesting small shops and premises along here, spreading out into the street and again washing everywhere and goods piled high.

By chance though, I came across the entrance to Huoshan Park. What a rich history I found there. In the 1930's and 40's a large number of refugees came to Shanghai and Huoshan Park became an activity area and meeting place for them. There were lots of information boards and monuments explaining their history. As in all parks there were lots of people sitting talking, playing cards etc. It looked as though it was still a popular meeting place and very interesting to walk round. There was a wonderful peace wall at one end.

There is now a Jewish Refugees Museum which was built in memory of the time during the Second World War when Jewish refugees sought sanctuary here. Between the year 1937 and 1941, Shanghai received 25,000 Jewish refugees.

The Jews lived a free and peaceful life here. Between the end of the Second World War II and 1960's, many left China and emigrated to all parts of the world. The life they had in Shanghai was so memorable, and they considered the city as their second hometown and called themselves "Shanghai Jews".

The story of the Jews in Shanghai begins around the 1840s with the arrival of the city's first Baghdadi Jewish population. This group was followed by the arrival of Russian Jews, but the story of Shanghai's Jewish past may have been less prominent if not for the remarkable story of the Jewish Holocaust refugees in Shanghai. The city took in and sheltered thousands of Jewish refugees escaping the Holocaust. Their story in Shanghai is one of struggle and survival but also a story of a people who continued to live and thrive despite major obstacles and serious deprivations.

Wealthy Jews from Baghdad had been living in Shanghai since the 19th century. Then, Russian Jews came to Shanghai before and after World War I. The third influx of Jewish immigrants, from Germany and Austria, arrived in the 1930s, fleeing the rise of Adolf Hitler and the Nazis.

Soon   after this impoverished group arrived, it was followed by the next group of refugees from Poland and Lithuania in 1941. This group were able to bring some of their possessions with them. Belonging to this group was Nina Wertans whose story is well publicised.

Nina Admoni (née Wertans) was six when Germany invaded her native Poland. Fleeing falling bombs and seeing starving people beg for food along the Trans-

Siberian Railway were some of her first encounters with World War II.

When the war first started, Nina was supposed to go to Vilnius, because that's where her mother was from and where her grandfather was a leader in the Jewish community. So the family drove to Vilnius but the Soviets entered the area fairly soon afterwards. Her father was considered a capitalist so life was difficult for them. They looked for a way out, and heard that a Japanese Consul in Lithuania, a man named Chiune Sugihara, was issuing transit visas for Jews through Japan. By going against orders and issuing Jews such visas, Sugihara saved more than 3,000 people.

But in order to get a transit visa, you need an end visa, Her parents managed to receive a paper from the Dutch Consul that stated that in order to go to Curaçao, a former Dutch island off the coast of Venezuela, they did not need an entry visa. This document essentially served as an end visa for her family, and others, because it provided them with a destination.

On the basis of that piece of paper, the Japanese Consul gave them a transit visa (in 1940), and they also got an exit visa from the Soviets. This was difficult to do at the time because people could not come and go as they pleased.

They took a train to Moscow, and then the Trans-Siberian Railway to Vladivostok, a 10-day trip. When the train stopped along the route people banged on the windows, begging for food. It was apparently a very distressing and sad time for Nina.

The family then took a ship from Vladivostok to Suruga, a Japanese port and then to Kobe, one of Japan's main cities. After just a few months, the local authorities reminded them that they were in Kobe on a transit visa only. They had to move on. The only place that would receive them was the open city of Shanghai.

Nina's family first moved to the French Concession. They lived on Avenue Joffre but by late 1943, the Germans told the Japanese that the Polish Jews were "stateless" as Poland no longer existed as it was under German rule. The Germans demanded that Shanghai's "stateless Jews" be moved to a designated area, where the poor German and Austrian Jewish refugees already lived. Life in the designated area — the ghetto –was harsh but it was safe.

Nina, as a young girl, was free to leave the area and play with her friends; her father, on the other hand, was not allowed to move around, and could not continue to work. People needed passes if they wanted to leave the designated area.

As he now had a lot of time on his hands, he taught his daughter geography, history, mathematics, and literature and that was how she was educated. Although she didn't speak Chinese she enjoyed playing with her Chinese friends and eventually attended the excellent Shanghai Jewish School.

While war destroyed the lives of so many children in distant Europe, Nina did not know the extent of the horrors at the start of the Holocaust — and if her parents did, they shielded her from knowing the full details. She does still remember the American B-29 planes' bombardment of Shanghai, several years after Pearl Harbour.

So thanks to good fortune and kindness, Nina's childhood years in Shanghai were a world apart from the horrors of Europe. She played hopscotch with her Chinese and Jewish friends and wandered along the Bund, to and from school each day.

Finding Huoshan Park so near to the hotel had enabled me to find out so much about Shanghai's history. It was while I was on my wander I noticed all of the little alleys and many older houses. These were more of the Shanghai nongtangs, the back passageways that combine traditional architectural design with modern Western architecture, giving an atmosphere that you will find in very few other places. These nongtangs have been around since the 1920s, and many of their original inhabitants still live there.

It was a really pretty park built on the themes of a Chinese garden again. Everything about them is really tasteful. I don't know who looks after the gardens but they were very well kept. As I wandered around people were staring at me, not in a bad way but it does take some getting used to. I didn't see any other European people during my wander at all, so I was bit of an exhibit myself.

Huangpu River cruise

After regrouping at the hotel I was out again for dinner followed by a cruise on the Huangpu River. There were long queues for this as it is a popular tourist attraction.

The Huangpu River is 114 kilometres (71miles) long and 400 meters (0.25 miles) wide. It is a branch of the lower reaches of the Yangtze River. It is ice-free year round and it divides Shanghai into east and west. On the West Bank is The Bund and on the east is the Pudong area. There are ships from all over the world on the river.

Cruising on the Huangpu River has become something most visitors do when they come to Shanghai. Large cruise ships also dock here as part of their journey. When the sun sets the river is coloured by the glittery neon lights from the buildings on its banks.

Shanghai has the largest container port in the world. The port handles the cargo coming out of the interior from Nanjing and other Yangzi River ports, including Chongqing which is 2,415km /1,500 miles away in Sichuan Province.

So it was back to the river but this time to see it from the water. It was great to see both sides, The Bund on

51

one side and the Pudong area on the other, both looking spectacular with the lights glistening in the water. It was rather windy so I expected a bit of a rough ride.

Ships from all over the world dot the river and the wharfs are busy. When the sun sets, the river is veiled in the glittery neon lights on its banks. Cruising on the river in the evening, visitors can experience its silence and beauty under the moonlight.

So cruising on the Huangpu River has become very popular for visitors in Shanghai and it was certainly very busy. Cruise ships vary in size, decoration and amenities, with the most luxurious offering air conditioning, conference rooms, banquet halls, bars and television.

While queuing to go on the cruise I witnessed how the Chinese queue. Basically they don't, they just all push and shove and try to get on first. It was quite daunting at first and so unexpected, but I got there. The next crush was when they were all trying to get good seats and views. The other noticeable aggravation were the selfie sticks. Millions of them seemed to appear over your shoulder just as you were trying to get the view to take a picture. However I survived.

Leaving here it was straight back to the hotel as I had to pack and be ready to leave early in the morning for Wuzhen, where I was going to spend the following day and night. During the night I heard fireworks going off and it reminded me of the four great inventions that China likes to take credit for. I had come across these when reading up before coming to China.

These are inventions from ancient China that are celebrated in Chinese culture for their historical significance and as symbols of ancient China's advanced science and technology.

They are;   1. Compass

                 2. Gunpowder

                 3. Papermaking

                 4. Printing

The concept of the Four Great Inventions actually originated from the West. Three of these Great Inventions being the printing press, firearms, and the nautical compass were originally ascribed to Europe, and specifically to Germany in the case of the printing press and firearms. However after reports by Portuguese sailors and Spanish missionaries began to filter back to Europe beginning in the 1530s, the notion that these inventions had existed for centuries in China took hold.

Compass

The earliest reference to a magnetic device used as a "direction finder" is in a Song Dynasty book dated to 1040-1044. Here there is a description of an iron "south-pointing fish" floating in a bowl of water, aligning itself to the south. The device is recommended as a means of orientation during the night. However, the first suspended magnetic needle compass was written of by Shen Kuo in his book of 1088.

Gunpowder

Gunpowder was discovered in the 9th century by some Chinese alchemists who again were searching for an elixir of immortality, they seemed to do this a lot. By the mid 14th century, the explosive potential of gunpowder was perfected. By that time, the Chinese had discovered how to create explosive round shot by packing their hollow shells with this gunpowder. We all know they love to use this to make fireworks.

Papermaking

Hemp wrapping paper was used in China around 100 BC. Papermaking has traditionally been traced to China about AD 105, when Cai Lun, created a sheet of paper using mulberry and other fibres along with fishnets, old rags, and hemp waste. A recent archaeological discovery has been reported from Gansu of paper with Chinese characters on it dating to 8 BC. While paper used for wrapping and padding was used in China since the 2nd century BC, paper used as a writing medium only became widespread by the 3rd century. The Song Dynasty (960–1279) that followed was the first government to issue paper currency.

Printing

The Chinese invention of Woodblock printing was at some point before the first dated book in 868 (the Diamond Sutra). It produced the world's first print culture. Woodblock printing was better suited to Chinese characters than letters which of course the Chinese also invented. Western printing presses, although introduced in the 16th century, were not widely used in China until the 19th century and they did not replace woodblock printing which was still used.

Wuzhen

Waterways play a very important part in this area of China. All the rivers flow from west to east. Near the coast the land is very low and some of it below sea level. Flooding has always been a problem, particularly in the east.

To counter this, a canal was built that went from north to south. The Grand Canal took one hundred years to build and is almost 1800 kilometres long and was finished in 618AD. It connects two major rivers and their tributaries, the Yangtze and the Yellow Rivers.

During wartime the high dikes of the Yellow River were sometimes deliberately broken in order to flood advancing enemy troops. As a result this sometimes caused disaster and prolonged economic hardships. The canal though has allowed faster trading and has improved China's economy. In the southern portion it is in heavy constant use to the present day. Since the founding of the People's Republic of China in 1949, the canal has been used primarily to transport vast amounts of bulk goods such as bricks, gravel, sand, diesel and coal.

Historically, periodic flooding of the adjacent Yellow River threatened the safety and functioning of the canal. In 1954 the river flooded killing 33,169 people and forcing 18,884,000 people to move. The flood covered Wuhan, a city of eight million people, for over three months, and the Jingguang Railway was out of service for more than 100 days. In 1998 a flood in the same area caused billions of dollars in damage and affected more than 2.3 million people, killing 1,526.

So from 1991 the Chinese were then looking for something that would ease this problem. A dam was the answer.

The Three Gorges Dam is a hydroelectric dam that spans the Yangtze River. The Dam is the world's largest power station. Except for a ship lift, the dam project was completed and fully functional as of July 4, 2012. As well as producing electricity, the dam also increases the Yangtze River's shipping capacity and reduces the potential for floods downstream by providing flood storage space. The Chinese government regards the project as a historic engineering, social and economic success. However, the dam flooded archaeological and cultural sites and displaced around 1.3 million people, and is said to be causing significant ecological changes, including an increased risk of landslides. The dam has been a controversial topic both domestically and abroad.

Millions of people live downstream of the dam, with many large, important cities like Wuhan, Nanjing, and Shanghai situated adjacent to the river. Plenty of farm land and important industrial areas are also built beside the river.

The Three Gorges Dam is not only the world's largest hydropower project but also the most notorious dam. The massive project sets records for number of people displaced, number of cities and towns flooded (13 cities, 140 towns, 1,350 villages), and the length of reservoir (more than 600 kilometres). The project has been plagued by corruption, spiralling costs, environmental impacts and resettlement difficulties.

The environmental impacts of the project are profound, and are likely to get worse as time goes on. The submergence of hundreds of factories, mines and waste dumps, and the presence of massive industrial centres upstream are creating a bog of effluent, silt, industrial pollutants and rubbish in the reservoir. Erosion of the reservoir and downstream riverbanks is causing landslides, and threatening one of the world's biggest fisheries in the East China Sea. Many scientists are concerned over reservoir-induced seismicity because of the weight of the reservoir's water.

The problems at Three Gorges though are not unique. Around the world, large dams are causing similar problems.

Because of the canal system many water towns grew up near Shanghai. I was on my way to Wuhzen which was 87 miles out of Shanghai.

The skyscrapers and housing blocks spread a long way out of the city but finally we came into the countryside. The area was very flat and there was a lot of agricultural land. All kinds of vegetables, rice, wheat and fruit were being grown. They have two crops of rice a year here and in the south three crops. The seedlings are started in a greenhouse and then after the first month put into water and then transferred to the rice paddy. It is known as the land of fish and rice. Seventy per cent of the food is rice and seventeen per cent of the land is arable.

In the past the people lived in communes and all worked for that commune. Now they are known as household responsibility teams. The responsibility has been placed back on the family. Therefore the more they grow or make, the more money they can earn. This means that some Chinese people have become quite wealthy. In the past agricultural produce was taxed but now these workers do not have to pay tax on the goods they grow so this has also impacted on their wealth.

It has also created what they call free labour. If there were too many people to work on a family plot then spare workers could move to the cities to find work. This has led to more movement especially of younger people to the cities creating a dynamic economy and mix of people.

After the economic reforms of the 1980's ambitious city dwellers weren't happy that the peasants in the country were getting rich while they worked for a poor state salary. Twenty years ago it was out of the question to even think of earning more than the meagre state salary and private enterprise was unheard of.

 The Chinese government would provide all that was needed and your salary reflected your social rank. This has now changed.

We passed through three toll booths on the journey which seemed a lot for a distance of 87 miles, but may be common over there. I am not sure as I travelled by air on longer journeys.

So I arrived in the pouring rain in Whuzen. Among all the beautiful water towns south of the Yangtze River, Wuzhen has become especially noted for its history and culture. Original ancient town scenery like bridges, waterways and houses are well-preserved. It is one of the most famous ancient water towns in China and has a history of more than 1,000 years. The ancient Beijing-Hangzhou Grand Canal flows through the town, with smaller tributaries leading off.

One day and night was never going to be enough to take in all that Wuzhen had to offer but I did my best. One of the special features is that some of the houses beside the river are built on pillars to lift them above the surface of the waterway. Wooden or stone pillars are fixed into the waterway bed, crossbeams are fixed to the pillars, and wooden boards are attached to form floors. This architectural feature is called a "water pavilion". This is part of the original architecture of Wuzhen. These water pavilions are really on the water. They often had windows on three sides so people can have a wonderful view of the watery scenery. Mao Dun described the water pavilion in his hometown of Wuzhen, in his book Da Di Shan He said: "...outside the back door there is the river. Standing beside the back door people can get water by hanged tubs. In my dreams I can still hear the sound of the boats floating in the air..."

Water pavilions are only present in the water town of Wuzhen and they give this place an elegant, cultural charm and are part of the spirit of Wuzhen. The whole town is a photographers dream. It is split into east and west.

The west village or Xi Zha has been rebuilt and renovated in the original styles with many unique architectural features, such as colonnades, small bridges, balconies, piers, wooden windows and doors, and grey stone walls and paving. With a main waterway and many side alleys, bridges, ancient docks and secondary waterways, it is really a fascinating place for tourists to stroll around.

It is pleasing to the eye and draws you into a forgotten time in China when waterways were used like road and rail, and life was simpler. This resort combines new and old really well.

Dong Zha or the east village is basically one waterway, sandwiched between two streets of original Qing Dynasty (1644-1911) houses. This is where you find the souvenir shops and restaurants and the various museums. There are several exhibitions showing the old way of life in this water town. In the peak season the streets are thronged with Chinese tourists (there are very few foreigners) and the water is busy with single-

oar boats carrying passengers up and down the waterway. Despite being given over to tourism Dong Zha is still inhabited by the original residents who go about their daily lives among the tourists.

Since its creation in 872 A.D., Wuzhen has never changed its name, location, waterways, or way of life. Traditional buildings remain intact today even after hundreds years of weathering. The mainly wooden buildings were built with no nails just perfect workmanship. Each piece was created to fit exactly. The traditional buildings remain well preserved within the town. The dense network of canal offshoots and wharves are where people built their houses along the water. Apparently there are more than 100 ancient stone bridges of different shapes.

Being in the middle of an extensive network of waterways it was once a transport hub linking all the surrounding areas. People living in the adjacent towns and villages used to row their boats here in the early morning to drink a cup of tea or to sell their vegetables and domestic animals. Gradually this developed into a thriving market. The people living in the houses could call out to passing boats, and they would row up to the house with whatever they were selling. I saw the postal boat go by, passing the mail and parcels to the people living there. It also still has a water market where you can buy goods.

As well as the hotels you may book a room in a resident's home and after shopping for vegetables at the market, you can come back and learn how to cook some local dishes. Less people actually live in the village now as many were paid to leave and given compensation.

Having checked into the hotel I went on one of the boat tours down the canal. It was interesting seeing inside people's houses as they backed onto the water and to see the different styles and shapes of the buildings. Then I walked along the streets to see some of the craft shops and museums. Shops were selling ornaments, kites, hand painted lamp shades, silk shoes, tea, medicines, all manner of goods. These all looked well made and they used traditional techniques. There was also the house where the famous Chinese poet Mao Dun used to live and whom I have already mentioned. Mao Dun is a revered writer in modern China, best known for the novel Midnight. His former home is located in the middle part of Guan Qian Street, where he lived his happy childhood. The home is a traditional Chinese style house built during the Qing Dynasty.

This was set up as a museum. It was surprising the amount of building and land there was behind the entrance and first courtyard.

Throughout history, people from Wuzhen have become well known in the fields of literature, history, and natural science, so it has a great cultural heritage. Wuzhen has organized art exhibitions for many local writers and painters and there is an abundance of folk arts. Interestingly it also holds the world internet conference each year.

Having existed for over a thousand years, traditional Chinese medicine is a treasure of ancient Chinese culture. The pharmaceutical history of Wuzhen is equally rich as a part of that tradition and the town used to have dozens of pharmacies.

Shadow Theatre

The performing arts in China have a long history and are very popular. These range from martial arts like Kung Fu to folk songs and dances that vary by region and area. They have constantly grown, developed and changed but are still true to the elements of the original art. China has been very adept at merging the old with the newer styles and also by retaining the main themes of nature and balance that they so value. As their history dates back over 10,000 years it is no wonder their art is so unique.

 While in Wuzhen I noticed that they still had a Shadow Theatre. Shadow shows were once very popular, certainly before recent times, and they were also used for religious and learning purposes. It is said that the Mongols who conquered China in the 13th century liked to watch shadow plays in their camps.

There were three types of puppet shows. These were rod puppets, glove puppets or marionettes on strings or wires, and shadow puppet theatre. This was mainly an evening entertainment and sometimes music or sound effects were added. It was simple enough for people to entertain themselves by moving figures against a screen or sheet illuminated by a lamp.

For the royal courts or the rich people, these performances would have been much more refined and performers highly experienced. Shadow puppet theatre was a popular entertainment in China for at least a thousand years, and it is still performed. Shadow play is a form of entertainment created by projecting the shadow of cattle or sheep hide puppets onto a screen. It has been regarded as the Chinese counterpart of the cartoon. All the semi-transparent puppets used in shadow theatre are handmade. The joints of the figures are exquisitely crafted and joined with string to ensure that the characters can move freely. Accompanied by traditional Chinese musical instruments, such as the flute, the pipa and the erhu, shadow plays are highly expressive and have captivated audiences from antiquity to today. The local shadow theatre troupes have been invited to perform in a number of countries, including Korea, Japan, Singapore and Germany, impressing audiences around the world with performances of distinctive Chinese character. Exhibits in the Shadow Play Museum do not only show the love of veteran performers for their trade, but also a general longing to return to simpler times.

Nowadays, performers use plastics, computer controlled lighting and machinery, and modern paint and dyes to produce bright and colourful shadow figures. They can produce images that are controlled by computers, and these can be used for animation and entertainment effects in shows. It is difficult for shadow puppeteers to compete with modern entertainment technologies for an audience, but some of them are using modern materials and adopting technology to help stage interesting entertainment in China. Shadow puppets could be bought in many of the shops.

That evening while staying in Wuzhen I went to see an outside operatic performance on the Xiuzhen Guan Stage. The stage was built in 1749. In ancient times, farmers around the town came by boat to watch plays. While the play was going on, the spectators would be in boats floating on the waterway. The performance lasted about an hour and was a story being told in song and music. Opera is very popular in China and a spectacle of both sound and vision.

Although I didn't understand a word of it, it was quite an experience. It was pouring with rain and the performer's flamboyant costume matched his voice. Apparently he was telling a murder mystery story in song. My guide thought it was very exciting. It is probably something I will never see again.

Chinese foot binding

One of the most interesting museums though of this Chinese water town is the Wuzhen Foot-Binding Museum. The museum is tucked away so I discovered it by chance. I happened to find the sign in my wanderings off the main streets.

The Museum displays 825 pairs of foot-binding shoes from various places in China.

Girl's feet were bound so they would be considered attractive enough for a good marriage. Women had little choice but to acquiesce in a society that was dominated by men, and the records actually imply that they were proud to do so.

At first, only girls from elite families in the wealthiest parts of China had their feet bound as tiny feet also meant that the girl would never do physical work. Her husband had to be wealthy enough to provide for her. Women were treated at the time as possessions and few women held jobs. These women solely served their men and directed household servants but did no labour themselves. It was less prevalent among poorest families where the girls and women had to work to survive.

The museum's several large rooms showcase lots of tiny slippers, boots, and sleeping shoes of Chinese women who had had their feet bound when they were children. Unfortunately as with many of my visits here there was very little information in English to take away or buy, so I had to look it up afterwards. Photography wasn't allowed in the museum either though exhibits did have English translations.

According to the Wūzhèn Museum, the process of foot binding started when the child was five. The girl's feet were broken at the arch, their toes fractured and folded over toes to heels. The broken feet were bound tightly so the feet would remain in a tight small shape. It usually took three years to remold the feet into a shape and size that would be admired by men. (More graphic accounts of this can be found on the Internet).

It is generally believed that the tradition arose when women started imitating the famous imperial concubine who was known for her dancing with her diminutive wrapped feet to make them look more delicate. Small feet then became synonymous with beauty. Regardless of its origins, it became fashionable among upper-class Chinese families over a thousand years ago, and it was only stopped in 1949.

At the start of the foot binding process, the foot binder would have to soak the child's feet in a solution of animal blood and herbs. Her toenails were trimmed and groomed, and her feet were thoroughly massaged. Once the skin was softened and the muscles were relaxed, the foot binder would curl the child's toes down towards the sole of the foot as far as the bones would allow. The binder would then curl the toes further so that the bones would snap. The child's foot then formed a kind of twisted fist. Presumably they had no access to any pain relief at all during this process. I am not sure how the binder would to be able to ignore the child's pain. Next, the arch was broken.

The girl's foot was then wrapped in long bandages, which had been soaked in the special recipe of herbs. With each winding the bindings were pulled as tightly as possible, drawing the ball and the heel of the foot increasingly closer and tapering the end of the foot into a point. The wrappings were then thoroughly stitched and allowed to tighten as they dried. Then they had to do the same to the other foot!

Afterwards, the girl's feet were periodically unwrapped to clean and then they were then re-wrapped even tighter than previously.

Once the feet reached their target size of 7.5 centimetres (about 3 inches), the unsightly bindings were then adorned with embroidered silk slippers. When such a lady went into society she became very sought after. Bound feet were considered to be sexually exciting to men, and girls who had them were much more likely to make a prestigious marriage.

In the Wūzhèn Museum there was a pair of shoes that had a drawer built into each heel. Fragrant powder was put into the drawer so that each time the woman stepped on her heel, a puff of sweet smelling powder was released.

An article by Alan Bellows, "Bound by Tradition", gives a lot of information about foot binding.

Although I knew about the practice, I didn't know that foot binding had impacted on so many Chinese women, or for how long. As it had continued from 937 until 1949 estimates think up to two billion women were affected. For most it meant a lifetime of pain and ten per cent of women died as a result of infection.

Now, it's hard to understand how the families and the women themselves took great pride in their small feet. The Wūzhèn Foot Binding Museum notes say that a woman's most precious gift to her groom was a pair of her tiny hand- embroidered shoes.

So it was a really interesting and thought provoking museum that was free and found in an unusual place.

The whole of Wuzhen is a photographers dream. It is so unusual whatever the weather. I stayed at the Passage D'Eau Hotel which was built completely of wood. It looked out directly onto the canal. In the room was a huge Four Poster bed with a beautiful, large silk painting above the bed head. It was the sort of room that you could imagine hadn't changed in hundreds of years. The hotel was designed for merchants doing business. Businessmen used to stop the boats, have a meal and stay at the hotel.

Shanghai Silk

Following a good night's sleep I returned by coach the next morning to Shanghai. The first visit of the day was to the silk museum. The first 30 minutes were interesting – the stages of the silk worm, how the silk is gathered and harvested, the spinning and the manufacturing process. They also showed how duvets are made and stressed the advantages of silk over other materials.

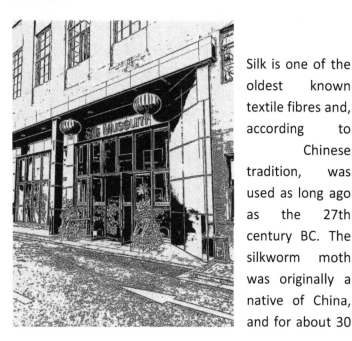

Silk is one of the oldest known textile fibres and, according to Chinese tradition, was used as long ago as the 27th century BC. The silkworm moth was originally a native of China, and for about 30

centuries the gathering and weaving of silk was a secret process, known only to the Chinese. China successfully

 guarded the secret until AD300, when Japan, and later India, found the secret.

Silkworms possess a pair of specially modified salivary glands called silk glands, which are used in the production of cocoons. The silk glands secrete a clear, viscous fluid that is forced through openings, called spinnerets, on the mouthparts of the larva. This fluid hardens as it comes into contact with air.

A typical adult silkworm moth is yellow or yellowish-white, with a thick, hairy body, and has a wingspread of about 3.8 cm (about 1.5 in). The female dies almost immediately after depositing the eggs, and the male lives only a short time thereafter. The female deposits

300 to 400 bluish eggs at a time. The larvae, which hatch in about ten days then feed on leaves of white mulberry, Osage orange, or lettuce. Silkworm caterpillars that are fed mulberry leaves produce the finest quality silk. Mature larvae are about 7.5 cm (about 3 in) long.

About six weeks after hatching, the common silkworm stops eating and spins its cocoon. The length of the individual fibre composing the cocoon varies from 300 to 900 m (1000 to 3000 ft). The silkworm pupates for about two weeks and then emerges as an adult moth. The amount of usable silk in each cocoon is small, and about 5500 silkworms are required to produce 1 kg (2.2 lb) of raw silk. The silk fibre is obtained from the cocoons by a delicate process known as reeling. The filaments from four to eight cocoons are joined and twisted and are then combined with a number of other similarly twisted filaments to make a thread that is wound on a reel.

All these stages were shown in the museum including being able to see and touch the live worms on the mulberry leaves. They were really soft to touch.

After the interesting tour there was the chance to buy. Prices to me seemed high but the quality was very good.

It was lovely to see the range of designs on the quilt covers. As well as bedding there were also paintings, clothes, scarves, fans, shoes etc. Almost everything you could imagine wanting to buy made of silk.

Shanghai Museum

That day lunch was on a floating restaurant on the river which was a bit different. The meal itself was similar to others I had tried. They seem to have certain specialities that all the restaurants serve but it was great to try different dishes. I enjoyed the lotus root, bamboo root and stalk, the egg plant and the white gourd, all of which I hadn't tried before.

Following lunch it was off to the Shanghai Museum.

The museum is located in the centre of Shanghai in People's Square which originally was where the racecourse was situated. It is a large museum of ancient Chinese art. Its style and presentation surround visitors with artefacts demonstrating ancient wisdom and philosophy. The exterior design of the round dome and the square base symbolizes again the ancient idea of a round heaven and a square land.

The museum has got eleven galleries and three exhibition halls. These cover most of the major categories of Chinese art such as bronzes, ceramics, paintings, calligraphy, sculpture, jade, coins, furniture, seals and costumes. It was one of the few places I visited that had some information in English.

I decided to choose a couple of art forms rather than try to see too much. The art section was wonderful with lots of different styles and also the calligraphy section was interesting, especially as calligraphy is such an old art form in China. Chinese paintings and calligraphy have very long traditions and unique national styles. Masterpieces from different periods and genres are featured in the museum. The examples they have on show, and there are many, really display how beautiful the art of writing can be.

Chinese calligraphy is widely practiced and revered in China. Chinese calligraphy and ink and wash painting are closely related, since they are both achieved using similar tools and techniques. Chinese painting and calligraphy are different from other cultural arts because they emphasize motion and seem to have a dynamic life of their own.

It seems to me to be about not just what is written but about physically how it is written. It can be found in many different forms and places. You often come across rocks covered in calligraphy. The local name for calligraphy is Shūfǎ in China which literally means the way of writing. In China it is still revered as an art form. Calligraphy has also led to the development of many other forms of art in China, including seal carving, ornate paperweights, and ink stones.

Chinese culture is the end result of the melding and collaboration of many nationalities. During its long history, minority nationalities have created their own colourful cultures. From clothes to textiles, metal wares, sculptures, pottery, lacquer and bamboo wares, the exotic styles of their artwork give a real vibrant range of material. It makes this museum a fascinating place to visit.

Sitting outside in the sunshine after my visit I had chance to appreciate what a lovely landscaped area People's Square is. There were lots of flower beds and fountains creating an oasis while all around are high skyscrapers and modern buildings. It was really quite restful. As mentioned it used to be an old racecourse where people socialised until the Communists came to power in 1949. In front of the museum building itself were eight imposing white marble statues of lions. Also in the square is Shanghai's municipal government headquarters building.

The Metro and the Jing'an Temple

My next destination was to the Jing'an Temple but to get there I was about to experience the Shanghai Metro.

The Shanghai Metro is fast and very punctual. The trains arrive and leave exactly on time. It operates to 13 of the 16 districts of Shanghai. You are separated from the track by glass barriers and gates which open exactly on time and exactly by the door of the train. We took the metro from The People's Square to Jing'an on line 2. The Shanghai Metro has grown continually but particularly during the lead up to the 2010 Shanghai World Expo. It now has 14 lines and 364 stations.

I thought rush hour in London was busy but have now changed my mind after experiencing this after work hours. Also trying to work out how to get out of the metro as there seemed to be so many choices. The difficulty is that all the signs are in Chinese of course which makes it particularly confusing.

Jing'an Temple whose name means the Temple of Peace and Tranquility, is a Buddhist temple on the West Nanjing Road. Jing'an District where it is located, is named after the temple.

It is known as the oldest shrine in the city, dating back even further than the city itself.

It was first built in 247 AD in the Wu Kingdom of ancient China. Originally located beside the Suzhou Creek, it was relocated to its current site in 1216.

During the Cultural Revolution, the temple was converted into a plastic factory. In 1983, it was returned to its original purpose and renovated with the Jing'An Pagoda being completed in 2010. The design for the temple strictly adheres to the style of traditional Chinese Buddhist temples.

Unlike its name, peace and tranquility, this small temple was garishly decorated and was very crowded and lively, not a place for quiet meditation. It was surrounded by towering office buildings and luxurious shopping centres. One unusual feature though was an underground fountain being built inside one of the buildings. It also has the largest sitting jade Buddha in the country.

The metro line station was really nearby and opposite was the Shanghai Star Park. As with all parks it was busy because most of the city living is in high rise apartments or above shops.

The park had lakes and rock and lovely corners like all their parks, laid out in traditional style. I also came across a huge stone sculpture of a rhinoceros! Not sure what the meaning of this was.

There was an old man by the entrance to the park painting on the pavement. He was writing a poem

apparently in beautiful calligraphy. He had something in the water he was using so it didn't dry out but remained damp so it could be viewed for a long time. A Chinese Banksy?

It wasn't unusual that he was writing poetry. Poetry was something I found in all sorts of places. It was sometimes written on large stones, on walls and on beautiful paintings.

Poetry is not only written but also spoken and chanted in China. It has always been held in high regard and has been a favourite literary genre for thousands of years. Poetry provided a format for both public and private feelings. My guide in Shanghai told me that the Chinese of his era did not speak about their emotions. He said that his wife had never said that she loved him, not because she didn't but because the Chinese expressed their love through the things they did rather than through the spoken word. Private expression of deep emotion is something the older Chinese people do not do. This is changing with new generations.

A high point of classical Chinese poetry was during the Tang period (618 - 907). This period was prolific in poets and also in poems and around 50,000 poems survive. Poetry was integrated into almost every aspect of the professional and social life of literate people, including becoming part of the Imperial examinations taken by anyone wanting a government post.

Poetry isn't taken overly seriously in the West, especially in the last two hundred years, but Chinese ancient poetry is still read and ancient Chinese poets are honoured.

Usually Chinese poems are fairly simple on the surface. Western culture, which was influenced by Shakespeare, Milton, and such poets, had a tendency to think of poems as ornate and elaborate creations made by a few men of genius. The Chinese had a tendency to think of poems as something written by ordinary people for the eyes of other humans. Usually the poems deal with the agricultural cycle, courtship and marriage or dynastic concerns.

Each poem is usually composed of lines of four syllables, usually with rhymed endings in the original Chinese. The poetic principle organizing the poem is often one of contrast. Often Chinese poetry will link a natural scene with a social or personal situation.

Returning by metro again I had dinner in the city. The food in Shanghai tends to be sweeter than other parts of China. As it sits just south of the Yangtze River and at the mouth of the Huangpu, it has a lot of freshwater fish and shellfish. These are only delicately seasoned and don't overpower the fish. Steamed crab is one of their specialities. The crabs are tied with string and steamed in bamboo containers. I'm told that the locals are quite fussy about when to eat male crabs and when to eat female crabs! I wasn't so picky. I was not always sure what I was eating as there were several dishes each time and you tried a little of each, much like we do here in England. We did get several chicken dishes (with bones) but I'm not sure if it was this famous delicacy found in Shanghai – Beggar's Chicken. According to my guide it is a stuffed and marinated chicken, sealed tight with layers of lotus leaves, then wrapped in parchment or waxed paper. This unique cooking technique produces very tender, juicy chicken. The bones just fall off after hours of baking and the meat is very tasty.

Shanghai food often looks quite red. I'm told this is because it is often pickled in wine. The food generally that I  had there was quite delicately flavoured and quite light, and as I said, slightly sweeter than elsewhere.

Following my meal I returned to the Ocean Hotel once more to check in again, only to shower and sleep, as next morning I was flying to the ancient city of Xian.

<u>Xian</u>

When it was time to leave Shanghai for Xian I had the option of taking the Maglev train to the airport. It wasn't a difficult decision to make!

The Shanghai Maglev Train or Shanghai Transrapid, is a magnetic levitation train, or maglev, that operates from

Longyang Road station in Shanghai to the airport. The line was the first commercially operated high-speed magnetic levitation line in the world.

The line runs from Longyang Road station from where I caught it, to the Pudong International Airport station. At full speed, the journey takes 7 minutes and 20 seconds to complete the distance of 30 km, although some trains in the early morning and late afternoon take about 50 seconds longer. A train can reach 350 km/h (217 mph) in 2 minutes, with the maximum normal operation speed of 431 km/h (268 mph) reached thereafter. It is impressively smooth with a real quiet power and it has a digital display in all of the carriages so you can see the speed building. I watched in awe as the seconds and speed built.

There was a feeling of quiet power. It's really sleek and

 tilts gently round corners. You notice the speed when you look out the window that is if you can tear your gaze away from the speed display. It vacillated between 430 and 431 km/h at its fastest. A great experience over too quickly.

Magnetic levitation, maglev, is a method by which an object is suspended without any other no support except the magnetic fields. Magnetic force is used to counteract the effects of the gravitational acceleration. The two primary issues that are involved in magnetic levitation are lifting forces: providing an upward force sufficient to counteract gravity, and stability: ensuring that the system does not spontaneously slide or flip so that the lift is neutralized.

So in just over seven minutes I arrived at the airport and checked in for Xian, a two hour fifteen minute flight. I left and arrived on time, passing through security really quickly. It was around midday when I was met in Xian by Ivy, a very knowledgeable local guide.

We set off for the city along with all the other traffic. Xian is a really interesting city and it is one of the ancient capitals of China. It is quite large and the capital of Shaanxi Province in central China. It was once known as Chang'an meaning eternal peace.

As one of China's Four Great Ancient Capitals it played a very important part in Chinese history. Xian's character is all about its ancient heritage.

Today they have really hot summers and freezing winters but I think at any time Xian would be a beautiful city to visit. The central city is pleasantly compact and its

grid layout within the city wall makes it easy to find your way around. The Bell Tower is the geographical centre of the city, from which four main business streets radiate, North Avenue, South Avenue, West Avenue and East Avenue. There are many further education colleges around and it is popular with young people and students. Actually, sightseeing in and around the city can keep visitors busy for a week!

Xian has many famous universities and hospitals. These included Jiatong University, which happens to be one of the best universities in China. It is one of the C9 league universities, the equivalent of the Ivy league in the USA. Ivy pointed out many of the medical buildings including a dental hospital and a military one. However she also said that if you need to see a doctor you had to go and queue at the hospital and you could be queuing for 2/3 days.

In Xian finding a doctor can be one of the most difficult things to be done, especially when there aren't many actual family practice centres in town and the idea of a family physician isn't something that has made it to China yet. While almost every area in Xian has its own general hospital that can treat everything from broken arms to skin rashes there are also specialist hospitals. They do though have an amazing service aimed at helping expats living in China. This is a 24-hour hotline with a doctor on standby at all times to answer any questions, make local and international referrals, help in translating with the local doctors and all for free.

It was reported in China Daily while I was there that the hospitals were gearing up for busy maternity wards as many older women would now try to have a second child having been denied earlier.

It is well documented and known that in 1978 China introduced the one-child policy. Whatever your views on this China has almost 20% of the world's total population and it was brought in to control rapid growth in the population and to ensure quality of life.

The policy allowed many exceptions for example ethnic minorities were exempt. In 2007, 36% of China's population was subject to a strict one-child restriction, with an additional 53% being allowed to have a second child if the first child was a girl. In 2015 this was changed to a two child policy taking effect from 1st January 2016.

However, back to Xian's history. Many past Emperors are buried here in Xian and its surrounding area. You see many dirt mounds as you travel out of the city, which are the tombs of ancient emperors and royal families. There are 2,000 ancient tombs near Xian and 72 buried emperors.

It is on the eastern end of the famous Silk Road. The Silk Road is an ancient trade route, and is actually the collective name given to a number of trade routes linking China and Central Asia. They were an important part of cultural interaction through regions of the Asian continent. They connected the West to the East, from China to the Mediterranean Sea.

The long and winding part of the Silk Road in Northwest China, has a history of more than two thousand years. Silk, the most luxurious fabric of all, was almost exclusively made in China until the 7th century. This precious commodity attracted Central Asian merchants, who in exchange brought horses, cattle, furs, hides, and luxuries, such as ivory and jade, to China. This was the start of the Silk Road. Silk was by far the largest proportion of the trade along this road.

It is though the immaculately restored and mighty city wall that dominates the centre of the city that we had to pass, with the traffic having to navigate through underpasses. This meant it took a while to get from the airport into the city as traffic was heavy. It has many ancient buildings, but the many modern buildings have been built in keeping with the ancient style, especially the roofs.

Xian has world class ancient, religious, cultural, and natural attractions, including the Terracotta Warriors and Horses, The Ancient City Wall, The Big and Small Wild Goose Pagodas, Huaqing Hot Springs, Mount

Hua, Banpo Museum, The Forest of Steles, The Great Mosque, and Qianling Mausoleum.

On the plains surrounding Xian are the well known Terracotta warriors, thousands of life-size, hand-moulded figures buried with China's first emperor, Qin Shi Huang. This was one of the highlights I had come to see, but not today.

We managed to get parked and our first stop was to see and experience the old city walls. You can ride around the city on a bicycle to experience the local customs of the street markets, the historical relics, and the old city walls. Although restored in places they are still very impressive. There were bikes and tandems for hire actually on top of the wall and you could hire them for a

day or half a day and cycle around the wall which is 13.7 kilometres. As you are high up here you get a bird's eye view of inside and outside of the city. It's the most complete city wall that has survived in China.

The wall now stands 12 meters tall, 12-14 meters wide at the top and 15-18 meters thick at the bottom. It covers 13.7 kilometres (in length with a deep moat surrounding it. Every 120 meters, there is a rampart which extends out from the main wall. All together, there are 98 ramparts, which were built to defend against the enemy climbing up. Each rampart has a sentry  building, in which the soldiers could protect the entire wall without exposing themselves to the enemy.

Looking down from the wall again I could see markets in the city and people doing Tai Chi. As well there were several souvenir stalls which were very competitively priced.

The Great Mosque

Back in the bus my next visit was to a Mosque. As I travelled I passed the famous Bell Tower. It is made of wood and is the largest and best preserved in China. It is right in the centre of Xian and traffic used to pass through large arches under the tower but today this is now a pedestrian subway. It was originally built in 1348 but was relocated and the structure altered in 1552. The tower had a large iron bell that was struck EVERY hour to tell the time. The bell can now be found at the base of the tower. There is now also a fenced park around the tower which I am told looks spectacular at night.

The street from The Drum Tower to Belyuan Gate in Xian is referred to as the Muslin Street. To get to and from the mosque I had to walk along this main food street area, also known as Huimin Street or Muslim Quarter Street. This was full of people selling their wares. Again there was virtually everything you could think of, in particular lots of street food. A speciality of Xian is belt noodles and I saw lots of this being made and stretched. I bought some walnuts that were being salted in what I can only describe as a life size food mixer. You buy them whole and crack them by hand. They were delicious.

There were crowds in this area and it was very noisy. Birds hung in cages and bikes constantly drove around you. It has become a famous attraction in Xian for its profound Muslim cultural atmosphere. If you are vegetarian, you may want to reconsider a walk through this street as it is a haven for meat lovers.

As Xian was the starting point of the ancient Silk Road 1,000 years ago this area originated because a number of merchants and overseas students from the Arabic countries and Persia went to Xian for business and to study. They then settled down on the present Muslim Street. They were called the Hui people by the locals. One generation after another, the descendants of the Hui ethnic people multiplied and lived on the street, and the number has now reached over 60,000.

I then arrived at The Great Mosque. The area has ten mosques of different sizes but The Great Mosque is one of the oldest, largest and best-preserved of the Islamic mosques in China. According to historical records an engraving on a stone tablet inside shows it was built in 742. It is really well worth a trip to see the Great Mosque, not only for its centuries-old history but also its peculiar design of mixed architecture of traditional Muslim and Chinese styles.

It covers an area of over 12,000 square meters and is divided into four courtyards. The gardens are landscaped and the further you stroll into its interior, the more serene it feels.

The first courtyard contains an elaborate wooden arch nine meters high covered with glazed tiles that dates back to the 17th century. In the centre of the second courtyard there is a stone arch. At the entrance to the third courtyard you see the Xingxin Tower, a place where Muslims come to attend prayer services. The fourth courtyard, the most important contains the Prayer Hall, the surrounding walls of which are covered with coloured designs. This Hall can easily hold 1,000 people at a time and according to traditional custom, prayer services are held five times every day, at dawn, noon, afternoon, dusk and night.

In China, this Great Mosque is the only one open to non-Muslim visitors. It was an absorbing place and there were two couples there, one getting married and another two having photos taken presumably for a later ceremony.

The Tang Dynasty Show

Following the city wall and the visit to the mosque it was already getting quite late and I was going to a special show and dinner that evening. I went to see the Tang Dynasty Show in one of China's premier cultural entertainment theatres. Established in 1988, the Tang Dynasty Palace has always staged the Tang Dynasty Music and Dance Show. It is the only cultural show in Xian which has a totally live classical Chinese orchestra.

The Tang Dynasty (618 - 907) was the most prosperous and glorious of all the dynasties and the show keeps alive its splendid culture and provides an insight into the peaceful life style of the period.

The show presented today is a recreation of the songs and dances performed during the Tang Dynasty according to historical records. It illustrates on stage the history, culture and artistic heritage of Xian. The performance showcases the costumes, music, and dancing of China's golden age. It is now an important tourist attraction for Chinese and foreign visitors.

In order to embody the characteristics of the music and the dance of Tang accurately, a lot of research was done reading historical books, checking records and monographs on the entertainments enjoyed by the royal court. They also set about learning traditional arts from folk artists and consulted experts on certain issues. Using these materials as a start they then visited many historical sites as a source of visual information to provide the backdrops for the performance. The costumes and scenery are wonderful and you can get some really fantastic photographs.

As an art form, the show has its roots in folk fetes, when dances were first performed by people as part of rituals of prayer for a good harvest or a better life.

Over thousands of years, the dances developed from a few simple postures or gestures to become delicate and artistic, reaching a peak during the Tang Dynasty. Unlike some other regimes, the Tang was open to outside influences and was willing to take in the best of various art forms of not only the past dynasties but also the ethnic groups in the northwest of China as well as central and western Asia. Thus a wide range of unusual oriental musical instruments and many techniques such as painting, sculpting, pattern and costume design were incorporated into the daily life. Cuisine and dining etiquette included singing and dancing. This was accepted by the Chinese, paving the way for the kind of entertainment that is now the Tang Dynasty Music and Dance Show. By combining poetry with the skilled playing of musical instruments, singing, dancing and also stunning costumes, the modern presentation is certain to give you an impressive view of ancient China including its splendid history, brilliant arts, distinct traditions and customs.

It was a splendid treat to see, full of colour, sound and movement.

The Tang Dynasty Music and Dance Show has now become a classic entertainment that has been warmly appreciated by audiences running into hundreds of thousands for more than twenty years. The production has toured many cities in China as well as numerous foreign countries such as Japan, Russia, Korea, Singapore, Norway, Denmark, etc.

As well as going to see the performance, you can also eat there, either in the auditorium itself or in an upstairs room. I ate upstairs after the show. It was typical Shaanxi food. They eat a lot of noodles here whereas it was rice in Shanghai. Pita bread soaked in lamb soup (Yangrou Paomo) is popular as is sheep blood soaked in vermicelli soup (Fen Tang Yang Xie,) which is popular with young and old people.

Chinese food tastes different in China to that found in Chinese restaurants at home. It is very regional and reflects the differences in land and climate. The flavours tend to be stronger and earthier.

So I had been on the Maglev train only that morning. I had caught the flight to Xian, seen the city, walked and the wall, visited the Mosque and the Muslim Quarter, been to a show and had dinner.

I thought it was time to check into the hotel. It was a beautiful hotel with lots of greenery around, gym, pool etc. However I was so tired all I did was go and prepare for tomorrow and go to bed. I was only there for one night so it wasn't worth unpacking. After breakfast I was off again.

There had been a couple of teahouses I would like to have visited but there just wasn't the time. One is the Fu Baoge Tea House which apparently is very popular. It is decorated in a pure Chinese style and has a thorough tea making procedure. It also has live music every day. Another was the Chang-an Tea House which also has live music and a genuine Chinese experience.

The Terracotta Warriors

As already mentioned though, it wasn't the city walls or shopping I had come to see and do in Xian. Today I hoped was going to be one of the highlights of my tour.

Chinese history begins in Xian when it served as the imperial capital for ten ancient imperial dynasties and a number of regional kingdoms. The first Emperor of China, Emperor Qin (from whom China gets its name) united the warring states in 221 BC and made his capital in Xi'an (or Shaan).

Emperor Qin became famous for unifying the warring states into what is now China, and then became the country's first emperor. He was also responsible for instigating the building of the Great Wall of China. The Terracotta Army is a monument to his power

The Terracotta Army or the "Terracotta Warriors and Horses" is a collection of terracotta sculptures depicting the armies of Emperor Qin. It is a form of funerary art buried with the emperor in 210–209 BCE and its purpose was to protect the emperor in his afterlife. The life-size figures are modelled on the First Emperor's real army.

It seems incredible now that the terracotta army was only discovered in 1974, and then it was by accident. Some local farmers digging a well broke into a pit containing 6000 life-size terracotta figures. In 1976 during excavation two further pits were found, both filled with more warriors. On the eastern side of the tomb a number of small pits have been found containing the bones of horses and smaller size terracotta figures of grooms. Since then discoveries have continued to be made at the site and to date the remains of nearly 8000 terracotta figures have been recovered.

There has been worldwide fascination in the discovery of the Terracotta Army and it is now regarded as the 8th Wonder of the Ancient World.

Work on the Emperors mausoleum began in 246 BCE soon after Emperor Qin (then aged 13) ascended the throne, and the project eventually involved 700,000 workers.

The terracotta warriors are unique. Not only are they life-size but each one is individually modelled in clay. The detail of the figures is astounding. You can see the construction of the body armour and even the heads of rivets standout. Incredibly the soles of the shoes of the kneeling warriors are even modelled with fine tread patterns. The hands and the heads of the terracotta warriors were made separately, and each head is reputed to be different and individual. When you look at them they are, they have different hairstyles, facial hair, clothing, buckles, shoes etc. There are so many differences just looking at the faces without going on to the clothing.

Although all the warriors were in the pits they had been buried in, many of them were in pieces and have had to be restored.

As well as restoring, the museum technicians and craftsmen have used the same techniques and skills as in the past, to re-create the majority of the warriors for The Terracotta Warriors Museum. The figures made in this way are in all respects identical to the originals

having been made near the Emperor's tomb in the same clay and fired in the same way as the originals. The warriors stand up to 2 metres tall and each weighs up to 300 kilograms.

Other terracotta non-military figures were found in other pits, including officials, acrobats, strongmen and musicians.

When you first enter the building and look down into the pit and see this vast army it is incredible, you can't

really put into words what it feels like. Many of the Warriors haven't yet been excavated. After the excavation of the Terracotta Army, the painted surface on some terracotta figures apparently began to flake and fade. The lacquer covering the paint can curl in fifteen seconds once exposed to Xian's dry air and can flake off in just four minutes. So until they have found a way to preserve the colours they are not excavating any more.

The same applies to the Emperors mausoleum at nearby Mount Li which has not yet been

excavated. It appears to be a hermetically-sealed space the size of a football pitch. It remains unopened, due to concerns about preservation of its artefacts.

Mount Li was a favoured location due to its auspicious geology, its northern side was rich in gold, and its southern side rich in beautiful jade. The First Emperor was aware of its fine reputation and chose to be buried there.

The Emperor had devoted his life to search for the elixir of immortality. He died aged fifty and according to a decree of the Second Emperor all of his father's ladies who had no children were ordered to follow the Emperor to the grave. Many of the tomb builders were also buried alive. In the Han Shu (Book of Han), the Emperor's funeral was described as follows; "thousands of officials were killed and thousands of craftsmen were buried alive in order to keep the tomb secret."

I suppose it is slightly less gruesome when you realise that the Emperor believed that life under the ground after death was a continuation of life on earth.

It is a really well set out experience. After buying tickets you walk through a lovely parkland area to get to the pits. As well as pits one, two and three there is an exhibition hall and information centre. You can buy food and souvenirs ranging from small and inexpensive to huge and very expensive. The farmer who discovered the site, Mr Yang, is now very famous and became a government employee. He is 82 years old now and until recently he used to go to the museum each day and would sign in person each guide book. As he was a farmer he couldn't actually read or write so he had to learn how to do this. He still goes some days but unfortunately he wasn't there on the day I visited. However I did buy a book that was signed by him.

In the open areas outside there were also many people trying to sell souvenirs. Discounts can be had up to about 50% off the asking price in many outlets and you are often offered 20% without even asking.

Instead of going back to the hotel now I was headed straight to the airport for my flight to Beijing. The good news was that the luggage which had been left at the hotel had already been transferred to the airport, had been checked in and all I had to do was collect my boarding card and go through security. It has never been so easy. However in these days of heightened security I am surprised it happened but it certainly saved me time.

The flight from Xian to Beijing was two hours and ten minutes. I arrived in Beijing at ten in the evening and transferred to the Radisson Blu hotel.

Now you might think that these large hotels would have staff that understood English but this was not always the case. I am not saying that they should have just that I was surprised (in a good way.) Although there are foreign tourists there are not that many, most are from within China. I rang housekeeping on one occasion for towels and couldn't make myself understood so I went to reception and they sent someone but when they arrived they started trying the taps etc when all I wanted was a towel! I made myself understood eventually. Another time I tried to get some fresh milk for tea but after two room visits I gave up and used powder. Generally though, it wasn't a problem. It is quite refreshing really that not everyone speaks English.

Beijing - Tian'an Men Square

Beijing is one of the world's truly ancient capitals and an extraordinary city. One of the tour highlights was a trip to the iconic Great Wall, built over 2,000 years ago to protect the Chinese Empire against marauding Mongol invaders from the North.

There have been many capital cities in China, some were only capitals of the region for dynasties that did not rule the whole country. Xian was the capital for early dynasties but Beijing was the last of the Imperial capitals and has remained so. In its early days before unification it was Jicheng or Yanjing, meaning the capital of the Kingdom of Yan. Its history has given it a grandeur but there has also been a lot of destruction of the old areas.

This morning though I was up early to start a comprehensive city tour starting at Tian'an Men Square. As I approached the square from Quianamen station the number of people and queues were phenomenal, I don't think I have ever seen so many people. Interestingly although there were lots of tour groups a lot of them were Chinese. It was predominantly the Chinese people who queued for hours to visit Mao's mausoleum. The building itself is known as The Memorial Hall of

121

Chairman Mao. It contains his embalmed body. His casket is raised from its refrigerated chamber and is on show mornings and afternoons. I couldn't believe the number of people who had come to see this.

Despite the problems and atrocities of the cultural revolution, many Chinese still see Mao as the person who has liberated them and given them a better life. Some of the elderly Chinese couldn't envisage that their life now could be so different from how they grew up. They were so used to having to make do, to being poor and having to bargain for everything that even today this is what they still do. Many Chinese come from the provinces to visit the Mausoleum which was built the year after Mao's death in 1976.

The square itself is huge. It is the sixth largest city square

 in the world according to Wikipedia. The Square was designed and built in 1651, and has since been enlarged to four times its

original size. It is surrounded by 1950's communist style buildings, gates and originally the old city walls. It is well known now as the scene of the student protests of 1989. Its function is that of the front door to the Forbidden City and was also used as the place to inform people when there was a change of ruling power.

Tian'an Men Guangchang means the Square of the Gate of Heavenly Peace. It is impressively huge and is bordered by important buildings. The Great Hall of the People where the National People's Congress meet is on one side, the National Museum at another, and the impressive entrance to the Forbidden City at the far end. Imagining passing down the length of the square we start with the Arrow Tower of Jian Lou and creating a double gate is the Zhengyang Men, a second tower which now houses a museum on the history of Beijing. This is followed by Mao's Mausoleum with its long queues of people waiting to visit, and then the monument to the People's heroes which was erected in 1958. It records episodes from China's revolutionary history.

Next is the flagpole where the national flag is raised at dawn every day and lowered at dusk. This happens every morning, exactly at sunrise, the ceremony being conducted by uniformed troops. The entire event lasts only 3 minutes. It takes about 2 minutes and 7 seconds for the entire sun to rise above the horizon, so the flag is raised very slowly taking 2 minutes and 7 seconds as well. It is exactly timed to coincide with sunrise.

The squad of troops emerge from Tian'anmen Tower a few minutes before sunrise, and they march to the flag pole in formation across a bridge in front of the tower. Sometimes crowds of thousands are there for important national holidays. The national anthem is also played.

Finally, across the square is Tian'an Men a huge Ming

Dynasty Gate which still has a huge portrait of Mao hanging there. This is where many photographs are taken. It was from here that Mao proclaimed the founding of the People's Republic of China on October 1st 1949.

From this spot if you go north you come to the Forbidden City and south is the Temple of Heaven. It is a great place to people watch and you could spend the whole morning just looking at the buildings and absorbing the history of the place. The square is filled with visitors, from home and abroad but the majority are Chinese from the provinces many of whom bring children to see the sights. People from all walks of life seem to congregate here.

The original city walls of Beijing were erected in the 1100's. During the Ming era (1368-1644) it had an outer wall with seven gates and an inner wall with nine gates. These gates are impressive buildings of several storeys, looking like impressive pavilions. Of the inner wall only two gates survive, one of them being Qian Men. The log gates now only live on as place names on the second ring road or names on the Beijing underground. The names of buildings are one of the things I loved most about China, they are so beautifully poetic and romantic, even if their past is less spotless.

Going back to the protests of 1989 it was one of the few times I noticed firsthand the impact of censorship. I had heard about the great Firewall of China and how certain sites were blocked. Facebook being a prime example of a site you cannot access in China. That aside, there is one subject that is absolutely, without question, censored, and that is anything relating to the Tiananmen Square protests and crackdown of 1989. On the internet in China, it's as if the event never happened. My guide was questioned about this and talked around it without really saying anything other than she was three at the time and discussed more about all that China was doing now to help ordinary people and how life had changed for them.

The protests began when demonstrators, mainly students, occupied the square for seven weeks, refusing to move until their demands for democratic reform were met. It started with a march by students in memory of former party leader Hu Yaobang, who had died a week before. As the days passed, millions of people from all walks of life joined in. They were angered by widespread corruption and were calling for democracy.

126

The military offensive came after several failed attempts to persuade the protesters to leave. Throughout the day the government had warned it would do whatever it saw necessary to clamp down on what it described as "social chaos". But even though violence was expected, the ferocity of the attack took many by surprise, bringing condemnation from around the world.

I also noticed in an extract from The Guardian 4th May 2016 that the last prisoner being held in China in connection with the 1989 Tiananmen demonstrations is set to be released later this year after nearly three decades behind bars. Miao Deshun, who was 25 at the time, was one of about 1,600 Chinese people jailed following a brutal military crackdown on 4 June 1989. During this hundreds of lives are believed to have been lost.

The families of those gunned down by government troops have yet to receive justice or compensation, and even today public remembrance of the massacre is outlawed.

May also marks the 50th anniversary of Chairman Mao's Cultural Revolution, which began in May 1966 and inflicted a decade of chaos and bloodshed on China, claiming more than one million lives.

However the entire area has incredible history dating back thousands of years. You could spend days in this area alone. To stand in the square is awe inspiring like many of the sights in China. The space, the masses of people, the buildings and the feel of the past is what I remember most.

There are security checks everywhere and Police randomly select people to check ID, so if you visit you need to make sure you have a copy of your Passport at the very least. You also need ID to enter the Forbidden City.

The Forbidden City

So I left the Square through the Gate of Heavenly Peace to enter the Forbidden City. This was one of the sights that I had really wanted to see from books I had read about the life and history of past Emperors. I envisaged it being the essence of Imperial China.

In 1961 the Forbidden City was listed as an important historical monument by the Chinese government meaning it was allowed special preservation. In 1987 it was nominated as a World Cultural Heritage Site by UNESCO as it is full of Chinese historical and cultural relics.

It is now recognised as one of the five most important palaces in the world. It is the best-preserved imperial palace in China, the largest ancient palatial structure in the world, and is a wonderful accomplishment of traditional Chinese architectural.

So as mentioned I entered the Forbidden City through Tian'anmen, the Gate of Heavenly Peace. It is right in the heart of Beijing and was home to 24 emperors between 1406 and 1911? The construction of the grand palace started in 1406 and ended in 1420.

In ancient times, the emperor was said to be a son of Heaven, and therefore Heaven's supreme power was bestowed upon him. His residence on earth was built as a replica of the Purple Palace where God was thought to live in Heaven. Such a holy place was certainly forbidden to ordinary people and that is why the Forbidden City is so named. It was originally called the Purple Forbidden City but is now generally known by the Chinese as the former Old Palace.

On entering the Forbidden City the gates are enormous. The colour and size are imposing and made a statement of power, as they are so large, heavy and studded. These are obviously telling everyone to keep out, the Forbidden City and all its delights were not for the common folk. As you walk through you leave the austere Square and begin to be amazed by the Forbidden City as it is a completely different world.

Passing through the gate, you then walk across an expansive brick-paved square to reach the main entrance to the palace at the Meridian Gate.

Entering through this Gate you cross Golden Stream Bridge, and arrive at the outer court. It is made up of two parts: the outer court and the inner palaces.

The outer court is made up of three main buildings, the Hall of Supreme Harmony, the Hall of Central Harmony, and the Hall of Preserving Harmony. These halls were where the emperors attended the grand ceremonies and conducted state affairs.

The inner court is composed of three more structures. the Palace of Heavenly Peace, where the emperor slept, the Palace of Union and Peace, where the imperial seals were kept, and the Palace of Terrestrial Tranquility, the emperors wedding room.

As well as all this there are six eastern palaces and six western palaces. These were where the emperor used to handle everyday affairs, and which were the living quarters of the emperor, the empresses and the concubines. These are now exhibition halls, where imperial collections are to be found.

The Forbidden City is huge! It consists of 90 palaces and courtyards, 980 buildings and 8,704 rooms. It is a majestic, palatial structure with some wonderful architecture and attention to detail. It is also very deceptive. When you see aerial photographs of it, it looks very compact but seems amazingly spacious and vast once you are inside it. Though you only get a glimpse inside rooms there are many treasures and interesting relics in the courtyards. One of these was a huge but very impressive bronze crane. Another was the three bridges across the courtyard and only the emperor was allowed to use the central bridge. The only other person who crossed it was his wife and that was only once on her wedding day.

Having been to the Tang Dynasty Show it was easy to imagine the spectacle of life for some within the Forbidden City. The numbers of people visiting here is unbelievable. I managed to get to the front at one point to look inside one of the rooms and then got stuck. I couldn't move to get away from the entrance such was the pressure from people behind trying to see!

When you can at last tear yourself away though and before the exit, you pass through the Imperial Garden. The garden is a real change from all the red and grey buildings that comprise the main areas, with lots of lush foliage. It also has a totally different feeling, much more relaxed and serene.

After walking through the garden it is out of the Forbidden City through the Gate of Divine Might. As you look back at it you can see how well defended it was and indeed still is. It is enclosed by a 10-meter-high defensive wall and at each corner there is a magnificent watchtower. Around the city there is also a moat, so it has always been well defended. It is a wonderful view looking back at it with the towers and the moat and the wonderful architecture.

Leaving an historic place of such opulence it was sad to see so many beggars just outside the city trying to catch the tourists as they leave. Some looked in a very poor way. There are a multitude of beggars in China. Some are children and some have debilitating injuries, diseases or deformities. Some need to beg but there are also professional beggars. These beg as a career to make enough money to live.

Also along this area were souvenir sellers. I was trying to bargain and watching traffic at the same time as the roads were very busy. I managed to buy three kites for my grandchildren with pandas on but in the process struggled to cross the road.

One of the big issues as a traveller was crossing roads. There is so much traffic of all types coming from all directions. Red lights do not necessarily mean that the traffic will stop but they may slow down and weave around you. If a car does stop then that seems to be the signal for bikes, both motorised and push bikes to cut in, so watch out! I found the best ploy was to stand near a Chinese person and go when they did, with them having most traffic on their side. I managed to survive - just! Like many other Asian countries they have whole families on bikes and rarely do you see anyone wearing a crash helmet. Though I didn't see any accidents they do have lots, and road safety is a serious problem in China. Xinhua news agency said in 2012 that poorly maintained roads and bad driving habits result in about 70,000 deaths and 300,000 injuries a year.

The number plates are quite interesting. They start with a character which denotes the province and this is followed by a letter and then five letters or numbers. Examples are 京C·A1234 and 苏A·1P234. They have different coloured backgrounds too.

Yellow plates are issued for larger vehicles, such as trucks, buses, and motorcycles. These licence plates usually have the designated area and then a letter on top of the numbers, as opposed to being beside it. Blue plates, the most common sort, are issued for small or compact vehicles. Agricultural vehicles use a green background with white symbols. Since October 2007, black plates are no longer issued for vehicles belonging to foreigners. Instead standard looking blue plates are now issued. However, foreigners are still issued a separate dedicated letter/number sequence to denote that it is a foreign owned vehicle. Licence plates for China's Police Service, Armed Police Force, and Military are in a white background, with red and black text.

Last year it was estimated there were 172 million cars registered in China. This obviously has an impact on pollution in the cities in particular. Smog wasn't something I particularly noticed while there but it is obvious in some of the photographs I took. In Beijing they have days when only odd numbered plates can be used and vice versa. They had a policy of limiting the number of cars in the centre of Beijing during the Olympics to try and cut the pollution.

September 2015 was the 70th anniversary of their victory during World War II and they had an enormous military parade through Beijing. The celebration included 12,000 troops in 50 different military formations along with hundreds of fighter jets. Leading up to the day hundreds of factories were shut and half of the 5 million registered cars in the city were banned from driving in the main urban area. When the day of the parade arrived, the air quality in the city of Beijing had dramatically improved.

An average day in Beijing clocks in on the Air Pollution Index at around 160 (out of 500), which means adverse health effects for absolutely everyone but by the parade day, it had dropped to 17.The day after the Victory Parade, cars were allowed to return to the roads and the Air Pollution Index in parts of the city immediately returned to an unhealthy 160 out of 500.

Back on the bus my next visit was very near, it was to the Temple of Heaven.

Temple of Heaven

The Temple of Heaven is a group of religious buildings that were visited by the Emperors for annual ceremonies of prayers to Heaven for a good harvest.

In ancient China, the Emperor of China was regarded as the Son of Heaven, who administered earthly matters on behalf of, and representing, heavenly authority. He therefore had to be seen to be showing respect to the source of his authority. So these ceremonies were extremely important. The temple was built especially for for these ceremonies, which were mainly prayers for good harvests. Once a year, at winter solstice, the emperors came here. A bad harvest could be interpreted as his fall from Heaven's favour and threaten the stability of his reign. So, it was important that the emperor fervently prayed for a very good crop.

On these occasions the Emperor and all his retinue would move from the Forbidden City through Beijing to camp within the complex, wearing special robes and abstaining from eating meat. No ordinary Chinese people were allowed to view this procession or the following ceremony.

In the temple complex the Emperor would personally pray to Heaven for good harvests. The ceremony had to be perfectly completed as it was widely felt that the smallest of mistakes would constitute a bad omen for the whole nation in the coming year.

The Temple of Heaven is considered to be the most holy of Beijing's imperial temples and has been described as "a masterpiece of architecture and landscape design". It was built in AD 1420 by the emperor Zhu Di in the royal garden.

Surrounded by a long wall and with a gate at each compass point, the arrangement is like many Chinese parks, with lots of straight lines and regular arrangements. However it does result in a balance and harmony that is very restful.

The Temple, which is actually an altar, has three main buildings. The Hall of Prayer for Good Harvests is a great triple-gabled circular building, this is where the Emperor prayed for good harvests. The building is completely wooden, with no nails. The colours on the wood under the gables is still very vivid. There is a lot of red which is an imperial colour.

The Imperial Vault of Heaven is a single-gabled circular building. This is surrounded by a smooth circular wall, the Echo Wall, that can transmit sounds over large distances. It is said a whisper can travel clearly from one side of the circle to the other but there were too many people to test this out!

The Circular Mound Altar is an empty circular platform decorated by lavishly carved dragons.

It is a tranquil place even though it is in one of China's busiest urban areas. It would be lovely to see it without all the visitors. By the time I arrived at The Temple of

Heaven I had taken so many pictures in Tian'An Men Square and The Forbidden City that the batteries on my camera had died and I had to use my phone camera. This was despite every night making sure I charged them ready for the next day. I found it so interesting that I took hundreds of photographs! I was thinking that I might never get to see these sights again. Over the trip I took over 2,000 photographs.

Leaving here I took rickshaw ride through the hutongs. These traditional buildings built around a courtyard are the old houses of Beijing. We even got to go inside one and look in the rooms. Although the rooms are small with the courtyard as part of the family area they seemed spacious.

Chinese Acrobatic Show

After dinner I was off to another performance of a very different type.

Most people like watching acrobats, sometimes just because they like to be scared and also because they are sometimes dangerous. We all enjoy the thrill but also we admire the skill and drama. Some Chinese acrobatics troupes travel internationally but they are not regularly seen by audiences outside the country.

While in Beijing there was the chance to see their amazing feats at a Chinese Acrobat Show. I went to see them at the Beijing Chaoyang Theatre. There is also the Shanghai Circus World which uses high tech lighting and colour effects. Apparently it costs millions to stage it, and also the Shaolin Temple which was made popular by the "Kung Fu" TV series. This one is more of a martial arts demonstration than a spectacular show like the others. This troupe has performed for millions of people from China and abroad including many state leaders.

The Chinese Acrobatics fall into two main types, martial arts style and circus style. Both are based in theatre, martial arts, dance and magic. These are all arts that are traditional to the Chinese. The martial arts

142

groups emphasize martial arts and artists often act out a fighting scene and perform with various weapons. Circus style shows are more like Western acrobatics shows. The individual performers and groups of acrobats do amazing acts of balancing, juggling, and gymnastics, and they are often amusing.

Chinese acrobats tend to emphasize balance and extreme flexibility more than the troupes do in other countries. This might be due to the influence of martial arts. One of the important aspects of the group we saw was the importance of timing, flexibility and coordination. They must practice endlessly to be so precise. Chinese acrobats focus especially on developing strength in the waist and legs which is the key to all precisely controlled movement martial arts exercises such as tai chi or kung fu where there is graceful movement

The show I saw had traditional Chinese music that was recorded, though sometimes it is performed live by musicians playing traditional instruments. China has recently been regarded as the country with the world's best acrobatic performances. The climax of the show is a group of motorcycle stunt riders who do amazing feats while riding around in a large sphere. They built up the tension as they progressed with more and more motorcyclists going into the sphere. I don't know how they avoid collisions, it was an incredible feat.

The Shanghai Circus World which uses high tech lighting and colour effects is also very absorbing. I didn't see this though. Then there is "The Legend of Kung Fu" Show in the Red Theater, Beijing. This is apparently the best martial arts acrobatics theatre you can see and the actors are excellent kung fu artists from all over China. The show combines kung fu, acrobatics, and dancing. It is produced to international standards by one of China's leading performing arts production companies. There is an English language show for foreigners.

As mentioned previously The Shaolin Temple was made popular by the "Kung Fu" TV series. It is more of a martial arts demonstration than a spectacular show like the others. However they still have a lot of acrobatic stunts being performed. The troupe has demonstrated their skills for millions of people from China and abroad.

The Great Wall

So this was to be my last full day in China and they say you leave the best until last. I was up early to travel out of Beijing to Mutianyu to walk on The Great Wall of China. It was going to be one of those days that you remember for the rest of your life. I had to travel about forty miles north of Beijing to get to the section of the wall, Mutianyu which I was visiting. As I got further out of the city there were lots of potholes in the roads and the land looked very dry with many dried up river beds. In the smaller towns there were lots of three wheeled bikes often with trailers and whole families on them. Also there were lots of pictures of Chairman Mao in the towns and villages. There was very little litter about and I also noticed that there were very few roundabouts. Lots of traffic lights but a roundabout was really unusual even in the cities.

I passed a lot of agricultural land, particularly fruit growing. It was also great to get away from all the high rise buildings. Most buildings here were only one storey high.

As I got nearer to the mountains the land became greener. There was still mist on the tops although it looked as though when the sun burnt through it was going to be a really hot day. There were one or two resort areas at the foot of the mountains, but these were on a very small scale.

Arriving at Mutianyu, there is a visitor centre with lots of photographs of the wall in all seasons. It is here where buy your ticket for the cable car. You can walk up but as I was only there one day I wanted to spend time on the top. I set off through the souvenir sellers to the bottom cable car station. The cable car delivers you almost to the top but you then climb the last bit on ancient steps.

Once you reach the top the view is jaw dropping. It's quite hard to take in the enormity of what you are seeing.

There is nothing that can really prepare you for the size and scale of the wall. You see the wall extend into the distance up hills and turning corners but you can't even imagine what its actual length looks like.It's quite hard to take in the magnitude of what you are seeing. It's impressive, it's awesome, it's incredible. So here's a bit about the wall. I have already mentioned about the first Emperor who joined lots of other smaller fortifications together, but little of that wall remains. Since then, the Great Wall has on and off been rebuilt, maintained, and enhanced.

The Great Wall of China is more than 2,300 years old and is actually a series of walls made of stone, brick, earth, wood, and other materials, generally built along an east-to-west line across the historical northern borders of China to protect against the raids and invasions of various nomadic groups. These walls were later joined together and made bigger and stronger, are now collectively referred to as the Great Wall.

Other purposes of the Great Wall have included border controls, allowing the imposition of duties on goods transported along the Silk Road, regulation and encouragement of trade and the control of immigration and emigration. As a defensive it was enhanced by the construction of watch towers, troop barracks, garrison stations and signals could be sent along it through the means of smoke or fire. It also served as a transportation corridor.

There are several estimates on how long the wall is but a comprehensive archaeological survey, using advanced technologies, concluded that the Original walls measure 8,850 km (5,500 mi). That's one long distance walk!

To put it in some sort of perspective its length would cross the United States east to west 6 times! I'm not sure if that is helpful or not.

The Wall is not actually a continuous line, there are side walls, circular walls, parallel walls, and sections with no wall where high mountains or rivers form a barrier instead. It was definitely continuous where I was though.

The Mutianyu section of the Great Wall winds along through high, craggy mountains for 2.25 km (1.40 mi). This section was one of the first to be renovated following the turmoil of the Cultural Revolution.

Although some portions have been preserved and even extensively renovated, in many locations the Wall is in disrepair. Sections of the Wall are also prone to graffiti and vandalism, while some of the bricks were pilfered and sold on the market. During the Cultural Revolution (1966–1976), many Great Wall bricks were used in building homes, farms, or reservoirs. Parts are also under threat of erosion from sandstorms and weather conditions. Various square lookout towers that characterise the most famous images of the wall have disappeared. As many western sections of the wall

149

are constructed from mud, rather than brick and stone, they are therefore are more susceptible to erosion. So it has got its problems.

One of the features of the wall at Mutianyu are the densely spaced watchtowers, there is one about every hundred meters on an ascending mountain ridge. Additionally both sides of the wall have a crenellated

parapet so that soldiers could fire arrows at enemy at both sides. Apparently this is very rare on other sections of wall.

In December 1987 the Great Wall was placed on the World Heritage List by UNESCO.I had only heard about this recently but there is actually a marathon run here. The Great Wall Marathon is an annual race held in May along part of the wall. Since it first start in 1999, the race has grown to several hundred participants. Aside from the main marathon, a half marathon, 10 km and 5 km runs were also held until 2012. 2013 marked the debut of an 8.5 km "fun run", replacing the 5 and 10 km distances. The course is much tougher than traditional marathons with participants challenged by 5,164 stone steps and many steep ascents and descents.

I can appreciate how hard this is as it is not flat at all. The short part I walked along had many steps and was always either going up or down. There always seemed a lot of steps up to any of the watchtowers as they were always on the highest parts. They were much bigger inside than I expected too.

The best time to visit Mutianyu's Great Wall is in spring (as I did) and autumn. In winter, it is chilly in the wind, and could be quite slippery on the wall when it snows. In summer, it is hot and there is full exposure to the sun on the wall. As it is in the mountains, the greens of pines and cypresses covering ninety percent of the surrounding area, means that the scenery there is beautiful all the year round though and you get the most amazing views.

Too soon it was time to return and take the cable car back down. There were some great views of the mountains on the way though. It was not particularly busy when I visited. I did get there early but this particular section is not quite as busy as some others but is renowned for the views. In the eyes of the Chinese people the Great Wall is not just a building but a symbol which carries the spirit of the dragon and shines with the wisdom of the people.

Having passed all the souvenir sellers again I was taken to a nearby restaurant for lunch. It was a really hot day by then and we returned to Beijing to visit the Summer Palace. This was something I hadn't read up about before coming and knew very little about, but as you will see I was very impressed. On the way there I passed some of the Hutongs that I had visited the previous day.

That night I shared a special bottle of wine!

The Summer Palace

The Summer Palace was originally built as a pleasure garden for the emperor's new empresses. It was first named The Garden of Clear Ripples, and was built by Emperor Qianlong in 1750 for his mother's birthday.

In 1860 it was burnt down by Anglo-French allied forces but in 1860 Empress dowager Cixi used navy funds to rebuild it. Perhaps not a popular decision! It has though made a luxurious royal garden for royal families. After completion of the renovation, Cixi renamed the gardens YiHeYuan which means Garden of Peace and Harmony which is its official name today.

In 1914 it was opened to the public as a private property of the Qing Imperial Family and then formally opened as a park in 1924. It's beautifully preserved and wonderful just to wander around. The buildings and features have such wonderful names. How can you not want to climb Longevity Hill or visit The Pavilion of Forgotton Desires and Accompanying Clouds? There is a large Pagoda style building that you look across to from the Forbidden City called The Tower of the Fragrance of The Buddha. It is one of the major buildings there and is about forty metres high with four tiers.It seemed to be a very popular spot and was full of visitors, possibly because of the view back to the Forbidden City.

As you wander in the park you come upon deserted buildings in the old Chinese style with paintings on the walls and empty courtyards. I found it easy to get away from the crowds by choosing to walk uphill away from the lake where most people seemed to be. I could have sat for hours in those spaces imagining a time long ago. I loved it here and would have really enjoyed much longer to explore. You could quite easily spend a day here and not see it all.

It is the largest and most well-preserved royal park in China, and is famous for its natural views and cultural information. It consists of a large lake, Kunming Lake and the land around it including Longevity Hill to the north - what a wonderful name.

There are over 3,000 man-made ancient structures in the park including pavilions, towers, bridges and corridors. It can be divided into four parts, the Court Area, Front Hill Area, Rear Hill Area and the Lake Area.

I have to say I found it to be one of the most beautiful sites in Beijing. The landscape, architecture, water, everything is a feast for the eyes. Even with all the people--and there were plenty--it was relaxing. I was lucky enough to be here in April so everything was in bloom.

Connecting the eastern shore of the lake to Nanhu Island is a Seventeen-Arch Bridge. There are three islands and thirty bridges in the Summer Palace and this is the largest bridge. It is the only way to Nanhu Island, and an important attraction in the lake area. There are 544 distinctive lions on the columns of the white marble parapets of the bridge and on each end is a carved bizarre beast which looks like kylin, an animal in Chinese legends. The biggest arch is in the middle of the bridge flanked by sixteen others. The beauty of the bridge can be admired from lots of different places in the park.

One of the most stunning places here though was the long corridor. It stretches virtually the length of the lake and is covered over so protects you from the sun. This was full of mainly older Chinese people sitting talking, playing cards and Mah Jong, playing instruments or just relaxing. There were marvellous paintings on the ceilings and all looking out onto the lake on one side and the hill on the other. There are about 14,000 impressive paintings of historical figures, landscapes, birds and flowers on the ceiling of this corridor, making it into a fantastic and stunning gallery.

Apparently it is the longest and most famous corridor in China. There were also a lot of boats on the lake, boat trips looked extremely popular. Some were even beautiful dragon shaped boats.

The Summer Palace combined political and administrative, residential, spiritual, and recreational functions within a landscape of lakes and mountains. All this was in accordance with the Chinese philosophy of balancing the works of man with nature.

Ninety per cent of the garden provides areas for enjoying views and spiritual contemplation. It is the culmination of several hundred years of Imperial garden design. The Summer Palace has had a major influence on subsequent oriental garden art and culture.

It was actually one of the places I loved best in Beijing, even more than The Forbidden City which had been one of my top priorities before coming to China. There was something about the atmosphere here, the detail and the falling into disrepair, shabby but beautiful at the same time. Nothing was precise and straight or angled here, it was much gentler but still with a magnificent history and visually stunning. The Forbidden City was precise and perfect, this was less regimented and more genteel. There was also much more variety here.

My trip was now coming to an end but I managed to squeeze in one more visit. This was to the site of the 2012 Beijing Olympics.

The Olympic Park

Beijing Olympic Park is where the 2008 Beijing Olympic Games and Paralympics took place. It covers a huge area of around four and a half square miles. The park was designed to contain ten venues, the Olympic Village, and other supporting facilities. Since then it has been transformed into a comprehensive multifunctional activity centre that is open to the public.

I visited the Central Section which is the main section of the park where there are lots of important venues and landmark structures. In the north-western corner, there is the Olympic Village, while in the southern part. I was able to visit the National Stadium (Bird's Nest), Aquatics Centre(Water Cube), Convention Centre, Indoor Stadium, and the China Science and Technology Museum. Visiting this area and seeing these iconic landmarks brings back the feeling and the spirit of the games, especially as this year is Olympic year again.

It was used throughout the 2008 Summer Olympics and the Paralympics and will be used again in the 2022 Winter Olympics and Paralympics. The Bird's Nest is a real centrepiece and covers a huge area and can hold 91,000 people. Its shape of a bird's nest, resembles a

159

cradle for new life, symbolizing mankind's hope for the future. The unique structure of Bird's Nest is awesome close up. The way the huge metal struts interact is really impressive. It is here where the opening and closing ceremony of Beijing 2008 Olympics were held as well as gymnastics, trampoline and handball events. The Bird's Nest Stadium is now used mostly for football matches.

Not far from the Bird's Nest, in fact just across from it, there is the National Aquatics Centre, also known as Water Cube. Its creative design originated from the arrangement made by patterns of cells and the natural structure of soap bubbles. The huge square box was produced by combining modern technology with traditional Chinese culture. In the past, Chinese ancestors believed that the sky is round while the earth is square, and that is the way nature keeps harmonious. The square Water Cube together with the round Bird's Nest, embody and interpret this idea. They are like huge works of art as well as being functional.

The Water Cube hosted the swimming, diving and synchronized swimming events during the Olympics. The building itself is not an actual cube but a cuboid. During the Olympics many people believed it to be the fastest Olympic Pool in the world as it was deeper than most Olympic pools. This may have been true as swimmers at the water Cube broke twenty-five Olympic records during the 2008 Olympics.

After the Olympics, the Water Cube was also opened to the public. Nowadays, The Water Cube is also the international advanced centre of swimming, sports, health-building services, and leisure activities. They have also opened here a brand new indoor water park featuring over 12 slides, including the Bullet Bowl, Speed Slide and Tornado which emphasize the fun element.

The water park takes up about half of the 12,000-square-meter complex and is now the largest in Asia. Lots of local people and tourists from all around the world visit both the Beijing Olympic Stadium and Beijing Aquatics Stadium

Outside the south gate of the forest park is the Sightseeing Tower. This is the 6th tallest sightseeing tower in China. It is made up of five independent towers, among which the highest is 810 feet high. These towers are built on steel frameworks and arranged in the pattern of the five Olympic rings. From a distance, the towers look like nails, hence the nickname Giant Nails. From the top of the tower you get a bird's eye view of the whole park. Apparently the Olympic Stadium is one

of the most popular destinations in Beijing but it was fairly quiet when I was there compared to the rest of Beijing. Since the 2008

Olympics, the stadium has been open to the public and has become one of the new landmarks in Beijing.

Outside the Olympic Park I did some last minute souvenir buying as there were some shops by the entrance. They had some lovely silk scarves and fans and I bought some to take home. The next shop though was much more interesting. It was a herbalist that mixed and sold all sorts of potions but also had some beautiful hand painted snuff bottles. It was these I wanted to look at as I have a small collection of old scent bottles and I thought one might go well with them. Of course once in the shop he had me smelling all sorts of snuff as that was mainly what he mixed and sold. They don't call it snuff but Biyan.

Biyan is a special preparation made with finely ground, high quality tobacco to which is added medicinal materials including rare and precious flowers and herbs according to the leaflet. These are stored in small containers or bottles and which then last for years or decades. These can then be sniffed up the nasal cavity. They call it smelling medicine in China. There is no smoke, tar or carbon monoxide produced from snuff and it doesn't damage the lungs, mouth or teeth.

His different mixtures were for the relief and control of the following ailments.

1. Helping to remove driving fatigue and absentmindedness.
2. Excessive drinking and unconsciousness.
3. Staying up late to study, work or entertainment.
4. Staying up late to play mah-jong, work on the computer or overworking.
5. Being tired from a long flight or train journey.
6. Clearing the nasal passage and gas, alleviating nasal obstruction.
7. Reducing headaches and migraines.
8. Improving eyesight, clearing away heat-fire, and relieving anxiety.
9. Allowed to be used in public spaces where smoking is banned.

So after duly sniffing a few I looked at the bottles. The price on them was 100 yuan. We had difficulty bargaining here as we didn't understand each other but with the help of a calculator we agreed on 50 yuan. I was happy with this but then pushed a bit further and asked if I could have it filled with snuff too for the price. He said no but he did it! It is a beautiful little white bottle with painted flowers on it and the lid inside holds a tiny spoon to get the snuff out. The type I had must have been number 6 as it smells just like Vic and does clear the passages. It was a really interesting half hour I had spent there and all for £5!

Generally Chinese medicine and herbalism has a long history. Their health practices focus on nourishing the body, preventing diseases and lengthening life. Acupuncture is also an integral part of Chinese medical science.

On leaving the Olympic Park area I passed a huge and imposing building with a panel of rainbow effect windows and lots of flags flying. My guide informed me that it was the Olmpic Green Convention Centre. It had been where the shooting and fencing had taken place. It is now the major press centre and broadcasting centre during exhibitions and conventions.

My final meal that night was to a restaurant for some traditional Peking Duck. This is a famous duck dish from Beijing that has been prepared since the imperial era. The meat is prized for its thin, crisp skin, with authentic versions of the dish serving mostly the skin and little meat and it is always sliced in front of the diners by the cook. Ducks bred specially for the dish are slaughtered after 65 days and seasoned before being roasted in a closed or hung oven. The meat is eaten with onions, cucumber and sweet bean sauce, with pancakes rolled around the fillings. I also had pickled radish and hoisin sauce. These are traditionally eaten by hand.

The remaining fat, meat and bones may be made into a broth, served as it is, or the meat chopped up and stir fried with sweet bean sauce. Otherwise, they are packed up to be taken home by the customers.

It was delicious and the chef seemed to be carving forever. As soon as one lot of meat was finished some more appeared. As it is cut so thin it goes a long way but I was completely full by the time I finished. It was rare to have a sweet or a pudding but after the duck some pineapple and apple fritters were served. They were delicious too. It was a wonderful final meal.

Returning Home

It has been an interesting visit and I have seen so much more than I expected. Interestingly though China isn't geared up for tourism in the way we are. There are no tourist information centres and leaflets are few and far between, especially in English. There is a state approved China International Travel Service which was originally set up to cater for the

needs of foreign visitors but actually it just offers tours, tickets or taxis. Although hotels and restaurants have good international standards communication still poses some problems. English isn't spoken everywhere even in the big hotels as I found out. Trying to get some fresh milk to make tea one evening I had two jugs of hot milk delivered by room service. The waiter had no English at all but finally understood I didn't want it and took it back. I then went down to reception to try and order it again but the next knock on the door was with powdered milk which I already had. I gave up at that point and drank it the Chinese way. However not having everyone speak to you in English is quite refreshing in many ways.

Another issue was that of toilets. I knew that you often needed to take your own paper so I always had a supply of tissues with me. However away from large hotels and restaurants public bathrooms are usually of the squat variety, or if there are several only one will have a proper toilet. Despite this they were clean and well looked after.

One or two other little nuances were common. The Chinese have a habit of staring but it's just what they do. I found girls often asked if they could have their picture taken with me. I think they like to see foreigners as there are so few compared to the Chinese population. I think it was also to do with my lighter coloured hair which is unusual in China. They also have a different approach to queuing! It seems to result in a lot of pushing and shoving. Spitting is also widespread even on buses and trains and in mid conversation which does take a bit of getting used to!

So I returned quite late that night after another extraordinarily long and perfect day with only a few hours to pack and sleep as my wakeup call was two thirty am, as I was catching a very early flight back to Shanghai and then on to London. Typically I hardly got any sleep as my mind was still thinking about all the wonderful things I had done that day. Was it only this morning I had been on The Great Wall? I had managed to survive my trip to China although I was unable to speak or read Chinese. I had managed to get around without getting lost which reminds me that at reception in all of the hotels it is good to pick up a card with the address on so that you can always get a taxi to get you back there as few of the taxi drivers spoke or understood English.

Arriving at the airport I had a very long wait to get through immigration and then the flight was delayed for over an hour due to bad weather in Shanghai. Apparently the weather had been wet and windy there since I left four days ago.

The Air China flight back was uneventful but again the air stewards were helpful and food great. I thought I had given myself plenty of time to get through the airport and across London to St Pancras but I caught my final train home with only ten minutes to spare. Arriving in Derby at 10.35 pm after a journey of 20 hours and 6,595 miles I was pretty tired. I had travelled a total of 14,966 miles in total.

It was great to be home with family again but of course I had so much to tell, hence the book. All I can say is that I would recommend a visit to China to anyone. It was so different and interesting.

The past is woven into the present and there is a sense of continuity in the people that comes from their civilised history going back over three thousand years. Although they have had a lot of political upheaval, one of the most contentious issues today is the encroachment of western values.

I was part of a tour but had gone alone, not knowing anyone until meeting the others in my group. All details of the hotels and the tour company can be found at the back of the book.

Accomodation

<u>Shanghai</u>

Ocean Hotel

1171 Dong Da Ming Road,

Hongkou District,

Shanghai 200082

<u>Wuzhen</u>

Passage D'Eau Hotel,

No 18, South Shifo Road,

Wuzhen,

Tongxiang,

Zhejiang 314501

Xian

Jianguo Hotel,

No 2, Huzhu Road,

Beilin District,

Xian 710048

Beijing

Radisson Blu Hotel,

No. 6A East Beisanhuan Road,

Chaoyang District,

Beijing 100028

Itinerary

Day 1

Fly to Shangahi.

Transferred to the Ocean Hotel.

 Night visit to the Bund and dinner.

Day2

Visits to the Yu gardens, the French Concession area, and the Nanjing Road.

Visited Huoshin Park.

An evening cruise on the Huangpo River to enjoy the views and the river traffic.

Day 3

A Day and night in Wuzhen, one of Shangahi's water towns.

Day 4

Shanghai Silk Museum and The Shanghai Museum plus a trip on the underground to the Jing'an Temple.

Day 5

Travelling on the Maglev to the airport for the flight to Xian.

A tour of Xian including the old city walls, Muslim Street, The Great Mosque, and a visit to the Tang Dynasty Show.

Day6

The Terracotta warriors and a flight to Beijing.

Day 7

A trip to Tian'An men Square, The Forbidden City and the Temple of Heaven.

A visit to the hutongs, and the Chinese Acrobatic Show.

Day 8

Visiting The Great Wall at Mutianyu.

After lunch a stroll in The Summer Palace and The Olympic Park.

Day 9

Fly back to Shanghai followed by a flight to London.

Tour Company

My trip was a tour booked through Mercury Direct called
"China Discovery Tour". I was with a group of 25 people
none of whom I had met before. They were a lovely group
of people and the guides both local and general were
excellent. They had so much knowledge and were so
interesting to talk to. The information and efficiency of the
booking was speedy and efficient. The hotels were all of a
very high standard and extremely comfortable. I had a
fabulous holiday and would recommend both the company
and the country to anyone.

List Of Illustrations

177

The Tang Dynasty Show Programme

1. Hua Qing Palace

Huaqing Palace is a piece of traditional music using traditional instruments. Located at the foot of a mountain in Lishan, it was once the palace of the Tang Emperors. It conveys the conviviality in the palace.

2. White Sleeve Dance

This is a kind of folk dance which was very popular at the imperial court in the Tang Dynasty. It originated from the Wu Kingdom, (today Jiangsu Province) and became very popular in Central China. Ramie was the main material used to make the long sleeves for dancing. The background song is "On the White Ramie" written by Li Bai, a famous poet in the Tang Dynasty.

3. Panpipe Solo "Spring Orioles Songs"

This music was composed for the Tang Emperor Gao Zong. The music portrays an early spring scene, willows, peach flowers and hundreds of birds singing in the bright sun.

4.   Spring Outing

This is a piece of famous dancing music for ritual
ceremonies. The music depicts a group of young girls
returning from a spring outing, dancing and singing and
wishing for a happy future.

5.   Prince Qin Breaking Through the Enemy Array

This was a Tang Dynasty Da Qu (Grand Tune), which
was first created as a large scale musical of song, dance
and musical instruments. It was a celebration of the
heroic valour and military prowess of Prince Qin Li
Shimin when he broke through the enemy array.

6.   The Red and White Peach Blossoms

March the third of the lunar calendar was the Spring
Purification Festival. It was important as people went
on spring outings and to be near nature. The "red and
white peach blossoms", was a famous dance that
portrayed the beautiful scenery of a sunny spring day.

7.   Trumpet Solo " Harvesting Chinese Dates"

This trumpet solo shows the happy and touching scene
where people, both young and old celebrate the
bumper harvest of dates.

8. Fairy dance in Feathered Costume

This is one of the most popular music dances. It was said that Emperor XuanZong was very good at music and poetry. One day he had a dream that he was touring fairyland in the palaces on the moon. He saw many fairy ladies in rosy cloud like costumes dancing and singing in the sky. When he woke up he composed a piece of music based on his dream and asked YangYuHuan, his favourite concubine to arrange and rehearse the beautiful dance and light music.

9. Percussion Show "Gossiping Ducks and Hungry Tiger"

This percussion piece was very popular around Xian. The music shows you through drums and cymbal gongs, how ducks play, gossiping and quarrelling at the waterside. Also how a hungry tiger comes down from the mountain, grinding its teeth in search of prey.

10. The Great Tang Rites and Music

This splendid collective dance reveals the grandeur and glory of the Tang Dynasty. It is the essence of oriental dance and music culture.

Reading Suggestions

Amitav Ghosh   Sea of Poppies
          ISBN 978-0-7195-6895-4

Amitav Ghosh   River of Smoke
          ISBN 978-0-7195-6899-2

Jung Chang   Wild Swans
          ISBN 978-0007-46340-4

Catherine Lim   The Teardrop Story
          ISBN 0-75282-593-3

Tan Twan Eng   The Gift of Rain
          ISBN 978-1-905802-14-2

Tan Twan Eng   The garden of Evening Mists
          ISBN 978-1-78211-018-7

Ting-xing Ye   A leaf in the Bitter Wind
          ISBN 0-553-81306-4

Further information on foot binding can be found in the following;

Alan Bellows   Bound by Tradition

Also by Lesley Gould;

Lesley Gould   Land of the Long White Cloud,

                                  -a journey around New Zealand

    ISBN 978-178035-410-1